Witches'
Spell-A-Day
Almanac

Holidays & Lore
Spells, Rituals & Meditations

© 2019 Llewellyn Worldwide Ltd.
Cover Design: Shannon McKuhen
Editing: Andrea Neff
Background photo: © PhotoDisc
Interior Art: © 2018 Laura Tempest Zakroff
PP. 9, 31, 51, 73, 93, 113, 133, 155, 179, 197, 217, 235
Spell icons throughout: © 2011 Sherrie Thai

You can order Llewellyn books and annuals from *New Worlds*, Llewellyn's catalog. To request a free copy of the catalog, call toll-free 1-877-NEW WRLD or visit our website at www.llewellyn.com.

ISBN: 978-0-7387-4954-9

Llewellyn is a registered trademark of Llewellyn Worldwide Ltd.
2143 Wooddale Drive
Woodbury, MN 55125

Printed in the United States of America

Contents

A Note on Magic and Spells

The spells in the *Witches' Spell-A-Day Almanac* evoke everyday magic designed to improve our lives and homes. You needn't be an expert on magic to follow these simple rites and spells; as you will see if you use these spells throughout the year, magic, once mastered, is easy to perform. The only advanced technique required of you is the art of visualization.

Visualization is an act of controlled imagination. If you can call up in your mind a picture of your best friend's face or a flag flapping in the breeze, you can visualize. In magic, visualizations are used to direct and control magical energies. Basically the spellcaster creates a visual image of the spell's desired goal, whether it be perfect health, a safe house, or a protected pet.

Visualization is the basis of all good spells, and as such it is a tool that should be properly used. Visualization must be real in the mind of the spellcaster so it allows him or her to raise, concentrate, and send forth energy to accomplish the spell.

Perhaps when visualizing you'll find that you're doing everything right, but you don't feel anything. This is common, for we haven't been trained to acknowledge—let alone utilize—our magical abilities. Keep practicing, however, for your spells can "take" even if you're not the most experienced natural magician.

You will notice also that many spells in this collection have a somewhat "light" tone. They are seemingly fun and frivolous, filled with rhyme and colloquial speech. This is not to diminish the seriousness of the purpose, but rather to create a relaxed atmosphere for the practitioner. Lightness of spirit helps focus energy; rhyme and common language help the spellcaster remember the words and train the mind where it is needed. The intent of this magic is indeed very serious at times, and magic is never to be trifled with.

Even when your spells are effective, magic won't usually sparkle before your very eyes. The test of magic's success is time, not immediate eye-popping results. But you can feel magic's energy for yourself by rubbing your palms together briskly for ten seconds, then holding them a few inches apart. Sense the energy passing through them, the warm tingle in your palms. This is the power raised and used in magic. It comes from within and is perfectly natural.

Among the features of the *Witches' Spell-A-Day Almanac* are an easy-to-use "book of days" format; new spells specifically tailored for each day

of the year (and its particular magical, astrological, and historical ener-gies); and additional tips and lore for various days throughout the year—including color correspondences based on planetary influences, obscure and forgotten holidays and festivals, and an incense of the day to help you waft magical energies from the ether into your space. Moon signs, phases, and voids are also included to help you find the perfect time for your rituals and spells. (All times in this book are Eastern Standard Time or Eastern Daylight Time.)

Enjoy your days, and have a magical year!

Spell-A-Day Icons

New Moon

Full Moon

Abundance

Altar

Balance

Clearing, Cleaning

Garden

Grab Bag

Health, Healing

Home

Heart, Love

Meditation, Divination

Money, Prosperity

Protection

Relationship

Success

Travel, Communication

Air Element

Earth Element

Fire Element

Spirit Element

Water Element

Spells at a Glance by Date and Category*

	Health, Healing	Protection	Success	Heart, Love	Clearing, Cleaning	Home	Meditation, Divination
Jan.		6, 13	20, 30	21, 25, 30	23, 28		2, 16
Feb.	4, 21		3, 7, 29	6, 8, 11, 14, 17	3, 16		24
March	6, 8, 30	25, 26	19, 27	29	3, 5, 10, 22, 23		4, 7, 11, 20
April	20	9, 12, 14, 16	1, 28	3, 24, 27, 30	11, 21	26	
May	3, 9, 23	17	8, 14	10	1, 4, 16, 28		6, 12, 13, 18, 30
June	1, 26	4, 30	27	2, 6, 9, 10	24		3, 7, 18, 19
July	9, 15, 27	10, 12, 29, 30		2			16, 19
Aug.	4, 14	10, 16	11, 12			2, 28	19
Sept.	5, 27, 28, 30		8, 16, 29	1, 10, 18, 20, 25	3		
Oct.	15, 21	2, 6		4, 13	20, 23, 30	10, 11, 14, 24, 25	3, 5, 7, 19
Nov.	8, 9, 10	5, 6		17, 20	23, 26, 28		14, 29
Dec.	7	10, 22	3, 15, 23	16, 18	6, 17	1, 24	2, 27

*List is not comprehensive.

2020

Year of Spells

January

Happy New Year! The calendar year has begun and even though we may be in the depths of winter (in the Northern Hemisphere) or the height of summer (in the Southern Hemisphere), we stand at the threshold of fifty-two weeks filled with promise. Legend has it that this month is named to honor the Roman god Janus, a god of new beginnings and doorways, but it is also associated with Juno, the primary goddess of the Roman pantheon. Juno was said to be the protectress of the Roman Empire, and Janus (whose twin faces look to both the past and the future simultaneously) encourages new endeavors, transitions, and change in all forms. Since this month marks the beginning of the whole year, we can plant the seeds for long-term goals at this time, carefully plotting the course of our future success.

In the United States, there are three important holidays occurring in January: New Year's Day, Martin Luther King Jr. Day, and Inauguration Day. Each of these days exemplifies powerful change and transition. The dawn of a new year heralds a fresh start, and whether snow-covered or bathed in summer heat, January offers renewed possibilities for all.

Michael Furie

January 1
Wednesday

1st ♓

☽ v/c 9:14 pm

☽ → ♈ 11:00 pm

Color of the Day: Yellow
Incense of the Day: Marjoram

New Year's Day – Kwanzaa ends

Glamour Oil

S tart off the new year by making a good impression. Creating a "glamour" in magic is to imbue yourself with a specific illusion or alter the impression you make on others. This oil is meant to draw out your most admirable, kind, and loving traits so others will feel them. After all, your vibe attracts your tribe, as the saying goes. Gather these ingredients:

- 3 drops lavender oil
- 2 drops patchouli oil
- 1 drop sandalwood oil
- 1 ounce carrier oil (jojoba, olive, or almond)
- A small jar
- A small rose quartz stone

Mix the oils together in the jar, and leave the rose quartz sitting in the bottom. Let the mixture rest under the waxing moon for three nights

to empower it. Add the oil to your everyday body wash so it gets all over you when you shower, cloaking you in a layer of charisma.

Kate Freuler

January 2
Thursday

1st ♈

2nd Quarter 11:45 pm

Color of the Day: Turquoise
Incense of the Day: Jasmine

A Theme for the Year

This is a wonderful time to choose a theme that you would like the new year to be rooted in and inspired by. This word becomes a lens to focus your actions and thoughts through as the year progresses. Some examples include *tradition, innovation, growth,* and *compassion.*

Contemplate what energetic quality you would like to bring into your life, and choose a word that embodies it. If you're unsure of what word to use, pull a rune or card, then meditate on its relevance to your life.

Once you have made a decision, write this word on a small piece of parchment and place it on your altar or someplace else where you will encounter it daily. You can also choose a symbol or make a sigil to represent the word.

Lastly, if you keep a journal or Book of Shadows, be sure to keep a list of each year and its related word for future reference.

Laura Tempest Zakroff

January 3
Friday

2nd ♈

☽ v/c 8:18 pm

Color of the Day: Pink
Incense of the Day: Mint

Winds of Change

The fresh-slate feeling of the new calendar year inspires change, and by calling on the clarifying power of elemental air and the ever-shifting energy of the wind, you can move through these changes with more awareness and momentum.

If possible, perform this spell outdoors where you can feel the air moving. Bring to mind the desired outcome of the change you wish to make, and focus on what you think and feel as you imagine already experiencing this outcome. Say:

> By power of air, my path is free,
>
> My mind awash with clarity.
>
> Wind at my back, I walk with ease,
>
> And each next step is clear to see.

The energy of air can shift your mental landscape when things feel stuck and introduce clarity when confusion sets in, so feel free to use this incantation any time you need a little boost as you move toward your goal.

Melissa Tipton

January 4
Saturday

2nd ♈

☽ → ♉ 11:15 am

Color of the Day: Gray
Incense of the Day: Pine

A Spell for the Mighty Dead

January 4 is the birthday of Doreen Valiente, the mother of Modern Witchcraft and one of Witchcraft's Mighty Dead. This spell serves as an invitation to the Mighty Dead to be a part of your rituals and to assist you in your magickal workings.

Carve the name of the individual you are honoring on a candle, or simply place a picture of that person under the candle before lighting it. Once the candle is set up in a holder on your altar, read something written by the soul you are honoring that has inspired you over the years. Light your candle and say:

*May this light guide you
to my sacred space,*

*And let my invitation be
one that you embrace!*

*Join me in my rights with
magick and mystery,*

*Knowing that forever
welcome you will be!*

Let the candle burn out, then thank the Mighty Dead for visiting.

Ari & Jason Mankey

January 5
Sunday

2nd ♉

Color of the Day: Amber
Incense of the Day: Juniper

Choosing Seeds Spell

With the new calendar barely opened, now is a great time to start thinking about the coming spring and what we wish to plant for harvest later this year, both in our gardens and in our lives.

Take some time and think about all the things you'd like to accomplish this year. Dream big! Then, on small, brightly colored pieces of paper that correlate with each goal (for example, you might associate green with money), write some keywords for each goal. Then fold the papers up tightly, creating tiny "seeds." Place these spiritual seeds in a bowl and mix them up while chanting:

*My gods, there are so many things to
do, help me see which ones to pursue!*

When the power peaks, scatter the seeds around you in a circle, deosil (clockwise). Pick up only those that your intuition tells you to, and save the rest for another time. Be blessed.

Thuri Calafia

January 6
Monday

2nd ♉

☽ v/c 7:08 am

☽ → ♊ 9:11 pm

Color of the Day: Silver
Incense of the Day: Lily

Wipe Away Negativity

Today is Epiphany. Many Christians believe this was the day the Three Wise Men met the baby Jesus. Today, some Christians, especially in Central Europe, chalk the initials of the Wise Men on their front door to protect their home from evil spirits. This form of protection magic is the basis of this spell, which you can use to protect yourself or your home or banish a bad habit. You'll need a small chalkboard, white chalk, an eraser, bottled spring water, and a clean rag.

First, bless the chalkboard by wiping it with the spring water and the rag. You may also say a blessing. Then write whatever it is you want to banish or protect yourself from on the board. Think about your problem for a while. Next, vigorously erase the board as you visualize the problem being wiped away. Clean the board again with the water. The spell is done.

James Kambos

▽ January 7
Tuesday

2nd ♊

Color of the Day: White
Incense of the Day: Bayberry

The Wishing Rock

Today is Old Rock Day, which celebrates petrology, the scientific study of old rocks and fossils. It's a great day to make a wishing rock, using the earth element for manifestation.

Gather these supplies:

• A rock or stone you've found

• Water-based paint in a color that contrasts with the rock *or* a white sticker and a black marker

• A sigil you've created that represents your wish

Bless and consecrate all the materials by holding them in your hands and blowing gently on them. Imagine your breath as a sacred cleansing wind that purifies them. Paint your sigil on the rock or draw it on the sticker and fasten it to the rock. Hold the rock in your hand for a few minutes, visualizing your wish as manifested. Repeat once a day from now through the full moon on March 9. Each day, take one small action toward the manifestation of your wish.

Then wash the sigil off the rock or remove the sticker. You can cleanse the rock and reuse it for another manifestation spell.

Cerridwen Iris Shea

January 8
Wednesday

2nd ♊

☽ v/c 5:16 pm

Color of the Day: Brown
Incense of the Day: Honeysuckle

The Scales of Justice

Today honors the Roman goddess of justice, Justitia. She is the personification of justice and is often depicted wearing a blindfold and holding a set of scales. She possesses these items to show her impartiality and fairness.

It would be appropriate to call on Justitia today to aid in matters of the law. Find an area where you will not be disturbed. Take a small piece of paper and write down the issue that requires intervention. Place the paper underneath a Justice card from any tarot deck. Say:

Lady Justitia, I seek your arbitration.

Bring swift and fair resolution.

Leave the paper under the card in a safe place where it will be undisturbed until the matter is resolved.

Charlynn Walls

▽ **January 9**
Thursday

2nd ♊

☽ → ♋ 3:43 am

Color of the Day: Purple
Incense of the Day: Myrrh

Anuket Invocation

Anuket is the Egyptian goddess associated with the yearly flooding of the Nile. Her many gifts include abundance, fertility, harmony, and joy.

Today, wash a handful of coins in water and white vinegar. Dry them in sunlight or with a towel, then place them in a ceramic or glass bowl. Fill the bowl with water, place a floating candle on top, and light the candle. Say:

Anuket, nurturing goddess of the Nile and the overflowing waters, I respectfully invoke your presence. Please flood my life with an endless flow of prosperity, laughter, and love. Open me up to receive, and help me remember that the more I have, the more I have to share. Thank you.

Allow the candle to safely burn for at least an hour. Dispose of the remaining wax, release the water to a moving body of water (preferably a river), and donate the coins to a charity of your choice.

Tess Whitehurst

January 10
Friday

2nd ♋

Full Moon 2:21 pm

☽ v/c 6:58 pm

Color of the Day: Rose
Incense of the Day: Rose

Lunar Eclipse

Ritual Cleansing

The full moon in Cancer today comes with the added energy of an eclipse, making it a powerful day to perform workings for cleansing and block removal. Facing the west, light two white candles of any size on a heatproof surface, then place a bowl of clean water between them. Using your index finger, draw a pentacle in the air above the water and say:

> Goddess of the moon, so bright and fair, descend now to bless your heir.

> Empower this water with purity, let it cleanse and bring clarity.

> What blocks I have are yours to find, removed from body and of mind.

> Come now, goddess, and make me whole, send your light to fill this bowl!

Take a clean white cloth and ritually wash yourself with this charged water, starting at your head and working your way down to your feet. Allow the candles to burn down completely, then discard the remaining water in the west at dusk.

Devin Hunter

▽ January 11
Saturday

3rd ♋

☽ → ♌ 7:16 am

Color of the Day: Blue
Incense of the Day: Sage

Leopold's Legacy

It's the birthday of Aldo Leopold, American ecologist and author born in 1887. Honor his legacy and strengthen your own magics with a charm for Earth and home protection.

You'll need a piece of natural material (round or square) about six inches across. Neutral-colored cotton or linen cloth, leather, or a piece of birch bark would work well. Use a pen or marker to inscribe a pentagram in the center of the material. Place a combination of the following protective herbs on the pentagram: rosemary, juniper, mugwort, wormwood, or yarrow. Use freshly picked herbs if possible. Add a pinch of sea salt and at least one of these protective stones (use a small one!): agate, obsidian, fluorite, or another stone of your preference.

Gather up the sides of the material, forming a small bundle, and tie with a green ribbon or thread of natural material. Walk the bounds of your property deosil (sunwise) while holding the charm, then bury it at the northern edge.

Susan Pesznecker

▽ January 12
Sunday

3rd ♌

Color of the Day: Orange
Incense of the Day: Frankincense

Cold Spell for a Clear Choice

Though by this time in the season we may be tired of the winter weather, its energy can be harnessed for a variety of reasons, such as this spell to make a decision between two or more choices.

Make representations of the potential choices that are freezable and small enough to fit in an ice tray, such as different-colored buttons, coins, or beads. Make a note of which item stands for which choice. Place each choice in its own cup of the ice tray, add water, and freeze. Once they are frozen solid, pop them out of the tray and set them on a sturdy plate. Hold your hands over the plate, saying:

A clear choice is what I need,

From indecision I shall be freed.

Melt the ice, dissolve the cold,

The first to be gone the correct answer will hold.

Leave the plate in a warm, safe place and monitor its progress. Whichever ice cube melts first will hold the answer you seek.

Michael Furie

January 13
Monday

3rd ♌

☽ v/c 8:42 am

☽ → ♍ 9:06 am

Color of the Day: White
Incense of the Day: Hyssop

Solar Citrine as a Winter Light

For those of us who live in an area of the world blanketed in snow around this time of year, and even for those of us who feel that occasional rush of bitter cold during the first parts of the year, those moments when sunlight emerges feel like a blissful reconnection to a warmer time of year.

To harness a little bit of this solar flare, acquire two pieces of citrine and wait for one of those sublime wintertime moments when you feel the sun reminding you of its imminent return. Focus your energy on that moment occurring either today or later this week, and you will be sure to take notice.

When you feel that rare solar radiance tapping through the cold, hold the pieces of citrine up to the sun and imagine the solar light filling them to the brim. Say something like this:

These stones are alchemized, magnetized, charged with the light of the conquering sun.

Keep one stone in each pocket throughout the winter season to stay connected to the nourishing light of the returning spring and summer.

Raven Digitalis

January 14
Tuesday

3rd ♏

Color of the Day: Black
Incense of the Day: Ylang-ylang

Friendship Spell

Focus on getting out today, because while this isn't necessarily a good day for romance or business, it is a great day for enjoying yourself with loved ones. For this spell, you'll need a shoe, a sock, an orange stone (either a crystal or a stone you paint or color), and cinnamon. A cinnamon scroll is best, but a pinch of powdered spice will also work.

When you get up in the morning, put the stone and the spice in your shoe, then say these words:

Whatever I do, wherever I be,

Wherever I walk, friends come to me.

When you're ready to go out, take the stone and the spice from your shoe and place them in a sock and under your bed. That's it! Wear that shoe with confidence today, and know that you've greatly increased your potential for meeting friends and creating great memories.

Charlie Rainbow Wolf

January 15
Wednesday

3rd ♏

☽ v/c 7:12 am

☽ → ♎ 10:43 am

Color of the Day: Yellow
Incense of the Day: Lavender

Melt Away Spell

Midwinter is an ideal time to clean house mentally and get rid of ideas and other things that hold us back. This is an easy spell to do to clear out something that's been bugging you.

Gather these ingredients:

- An ice cube
- A marker
- A cup or bowl
- Salt

Select a fresh ice cube from the freezer. With the marker, write on the cube (before it starts to melt) a word that represents what you wish to get rid of. Place the ice in a cup or bowl, then sprinkle salt on it as you say:

As this ice melts, so too shall this issue begin to diminish and fade away. I cleanse away that which I do not need.

Place the bowl in a safe place where it won't be disturbed, and allow the ice cube to melt overnight. In the morning, empty the water in the toilet and flush it away.

Laura Tempest Zakroff

January 16
Thursday

3rd ♎

Color of the Day: Crimson
Incense of the Day: Clove

Spiral Meditation

The spiral is an ancient symbol and has had many meanings throughout history across the world. The most popular interpretation is evolution, growth, and the revealing of hidden knowledge. Meditating on a spiral shape is a good practice to open doors inside your subconscious to help you better understand your purpose in this life and uncover important spiritual lessons.

On a dark-colored surface or black paper, pour some table salt in the shape of a spiral, starting at the center and working outward. Table salt often comes in a box with a pouring feature, making it perfect for this.

Relax and gaze into the spiral as you take deep breaths and let go of intrusive thoughts. Allow your vision to blur as you sink into a meditative state, paying attention to what sounds, thoughts, and images flitter across your mind. When you're done meditating, write down all that you heard or saw. If the information you receive doesn't make sense right now, it will in time. Scatter the salt outdoors if possible and ask for clarity.

Kate Freuler

⊕ **January 17**
Friday

3rd ♎
☽ v/c 7:58 am
4th Quarter 7:58 am
☽ → ♏ 1:20 pm

Color of the Day: Purple
Incense of the Day: Thyme

Harmonizing with Spirit

The four elements arise from and return to spirit, thus spirit can help us feel more integrated when we're experiencing elemental imbalance. For this ritual, you'll need a white candle in a holder and something to represent each of the four elements (for example, a stone, feather, candle, and water). Arrange the elements around you (right, left, front, back) in whatever way feels best, then sit in the center with the white candle.

Feel the elements, and notice if you feel drawn to or repelled by any of them, getting a sense of any potential imbalance. You can ask any of the elements for guidance in this space. Then light the white candle, and envision the light of spirit radiating out from the center, your center, and expanding to encompass all four elements, bringing them into perfect harmony within you. Open to receive any further insights, including ways to express this harmony in your daily life, before thanking the elements and closing the ritual. Be sure to extinguish the candle.

Melissa Tipton

January 18
Saturday

4ᵗʰ ♏

Color of the Day: Black
Incense of the Day: Rue

Money to Pay the Bills Spell

Recouping financially from the holiday season can be difficult, and by the middle of January, many folks scramble to pay their bills. This spell is an easy way to bring a little extra money in to cover those stresses.

For this spell, you'll need a small green candle, a one-dollar bill, and a needle or pin for carving your candle. Start by carving a dollar sign ($) into your candle, then anoint it with a money-drawing oil such as cinnamon, almond, or peppermint. Place your carved and anointed candle into a holder and set it on top of your dollar. As you light the candle, say:

Money to pay the bills,

Manifest by my will!

Envision all of your bills being paid, with a little bit left over for yourself. Repeat the spell daily until the candle is burned out, being sure to extinguish the candle when you are unable to keep an eye on it.

Ari & Jason Mankey

January 19
Sunday

4th ♏

☽ v/c 4:22 pm

☽ → ♐ 5:41 pm

Color of the Day: Gold
Incense of the Day: Marigold

Banishing heartache Spell

Sometimes we find ourselves falling for someone who, for one reason or another, is not available to us, yet we still must see them regularly. This can create difficult emotions, to say the least. For this spell, take cotton embroidery thread of the colors you associate with love, sexual attraction, and passion. (If there's overlap, use black, for the Mystery.) Braid these threads together in a length long enough to go around your ankle. While doing so, think strongly of your ardor for this person and chant:

With every step I take, with every choice I make, my ardor finds a better path, a more desirable fate.

Tie a knot in the braid for each reason the relationship can't work, then tie the braid around your ankle. Whenever you are with this person, make sure to point your feet away from them! By the time the braid falls off, your ardor should be banished, leaving the relationship comfortably platonic.

Thuri Calafia

January 20
Monday

4th ♐

☉ → ♒ 9:55 am

☽ v/c 11:46 pm

Color of the Day: Ivory
Incense of the Day: Clary sage

Martin Luther King Jr. Day

What Is Your Dream?

Today we celebrate the work of Dr. Martin Luther King Jr. Go to YouTube and listen to his "I Have a Dream" speech, which he delivered on August 28, 1963, during the March on Washington.

What dream do you have? Cast your circle and set up your altar with four green candles in holders and symbols of what can make your dream come true. Light the candles, call in the four quarters, and invoke the god or goddess who can send the elements of your dream to you.

Speak this invocation:

I dream, and dreams come true.

I dream and make my life anew.

Now speak your dream aloud. Describe it in the minutest detail. Take as much time as necessary so the Invisibles know precisely what you want. Speak the invocation again.

Remember that Dr. King's dream has not yet come true, although it's moving along. Your dream will probably arrive incrementally.

Barbara Ardinger

January 21
Tuesday

4th ♐

Color of the Day: Maroon
Incense of the Day: Geranium

Dream of a Lover Spell

Traditionally this was considered to be a good day to divine the identity of a future love. This was done by casting a spell that would reveal the image of a new lover during a dream.

For this spell, you'll need a pinch each of dried rosemary and thyme, a small square of fabric, and pink ribbon. At bedtime, lay the fabric wrong-side up, and sprinkle the herbs in the center of it. Tie the corners of the fabric together with the ribbon as you say:

*With a pinch of rosemary
and a pinch of thyme,*

The image of a new lover I shall divine.

Herbs of love, relax my mind,

Let me see a lover, sweet and kind.

Tuck the bundle beneath your pillow and go to sleep. When you awake, record your dream's images in a journal. Save the herb bundle, and use it again if you wish.

James Kambos

January 22
Wednesday

4th ♑

☽ → ♑ 12:00 am

Color of the Day: Topaz
Incense of the Day: Lilac

Thinking of You

In January 1673, postal service began between New York and Boston. In honor of this, take a few minutes to write a real letter or card (not an email) to someone you value with whom you haven't had contact in a long time.

Gather these supplies:

- Paper or a card
- A pen
- An envelope
- A pretty stamp

Bless the supplies in the name(s) of Mercury and/or Iris. In addition to being the Greek goddess of the rainbow, Iris keeps lines of communication open between the worlds.

As you write, focus on how much you care about the recipient. Let that energy flow through your pen and into your words.

You can keep it simple. Even the words *I'm thinking about you and wish you happiness* can make an enormous difference in someone's day.

Write the note by hand and address the envelope by hand. Attach the stamp, then mail the card with this blessing:

May this note brighten (recipient's) day.
It will!

Cerridwen Iris Shea

 January 23
Thursday

4ℏ ♑

☽ v/c 9:08 pm

Color of the Day: Green
Incense of the Day: Nutmeg

Dark Moon Detox

A dark moon is neither an inhale nor an exhale but rather the pause between the breaths. It's the perfect time to energetically detoxify and clear the decks for a fresh and successful new moon cycle and lunar year.

Cover a salad plate with sea salt and sprinkle dried sage over the top of it. Place a black candle in the center of the plate and light it safely. Imagine all heaviness, stuckness, and energetic debris within your body, aura, home, and life being sucked toward the candle and into the sea salt and sage, where it is instantly neutralized and dissolved. Relax and breathe deeply. Willingly release all tension, worry, and other unwanted emotions, feeling them drain from you and disappear. Extinguish the candle.

If possible, enhance this candle spell with physical forms of detoxification, such as clutter clearing, drinking lots of pure water, taking a sea salt bath, and/or eating lots of healthy, natural foods.

Tess Whitehurst

January 24
Friday

4ℏ ♑

☽ → ♒ 8:20 am

New Moon 4:42 pm

Color of the Day: Coral
Incense of the Day: Violet

Dream Divine-ly!

The dark moon is a term used by magic users to describe the time when the moon cannot be seen in the night sky, while new moon is used by astronomers and astrologers to describe the same period. The new moon stands opposite the full moon; it's marked by a deep sense of quiet and is often part of new beginnings and renewals. It's also a great time for divination and introspection.

Just before bedtime on this dark moon night, set up a quiet candlelit workspace with your favorite divination tool at hand. Put on clean nightclothes and wash your hands and face. When you are settled into your workspace, use divination to ask questions about your path, your direction, your choices, or other areas of interest. Immediately after divining, safely extinguish the candles and go straight to bed in a dark room. Your deep dark-moon dreams will bring answers to your questions.

Susan Pesznecker

January 25
Saturday

1st ♒

☽ v/c 2:06 pm

Color of the Day: Gray
Incense of the Day: Sandalwood

Lunar New Year (Rat)

happy Lunar New Year!

Happy Lunar New Year! Today marks the beginning of the Year of the Rat in Chinese and Taoist astrology. This year is also ruled by the element Metal. In these ancient astrological systems, the Rat represents a potential beginning of great new things. For those of us who have interacted with rats as pets (myself included!), we know that they are very methodical creatures who always look before they leap. Because today's lunar energy is a springboard of newness, it's imperative that we invoke clarity and stay true to our intuition throughout the year. Today marks the beginning of action and doing rather than thinking or pondering.

Take advantage of this energy by taking a handful of seeds (of any type) and going outside under the dark moon. Offer these seeds to the earth while speaking your prayers to the energy of Rat. Discuss your desire for success in various projects and ventures, describing the steps you will take to achieve your goals. Meditate for a while and imagine a mischief of rats (that's the term for a group of rats!) coming to feast on the seeds. If you wish, conclude the night with a firework or light a candle for the new year.

Raven Digitalis

 January 26
Sunday

1st ≈

☽ → ♓ 6:44 pm

Color of the Day: Yellow
Incense of the Day: Heliotrope

Magical Alignment

Since winter can take its toll on the body and mind, a bit of self-care could be in order. To begin, take a relaxing shower or bath and then lie down. Close your eyes and concentrate on the energy of your body. Mentally channel your energy in calming waves moving slowly up and down your whole body, clearing any blockages and soothing any weak spots.

Envision your body being clear of imbalance, feeling lighter and strong, and declare that you are realigned and magically renewed. If you work with the chakra system, visualize each of the energy centers as glowing brightly with power. Once you feel fully clear and aligned, disperse any excess energy by mentally sending it out through your hands and/or feet and into the ground, then open your eyes.

Michael Furie

January 27
Monday

1st ♓

Color of the Day: Lavender
Incense of the Day: Rosemary

Opening the Lines of Communication

With the sun still in the early stages of its journey through Aquarius and the moon riding high in Pisces, today is an excellent day to perform workings to strengthen relationships of all kinds that lack a clear emotional connection. Cast this spell to open the lines of communication between you and a loved one.

Dress a yellow candle with lavender essential oil and place it on a heatproof surface. Light it while facing the north. Visualize the person you want to have a better connection with and say:

From the heart, by the soul,
of the mind; a way through
this, we shall find.

I open the road to understanding,
our connection is notwithstanding.

Speak the truth and open wide,
from my spell you cannot hide.

I draw a line from me to you,
to usher in a breakthrough.

Allow the candle to burn down completely.

Devin Hunter

 January 28
Tuesday

1st ♓

☽ v/c 8:08 pm

Color of the Day: Scarlet
Incense of the Day: Ginger

Good Vibes Candle

For this spell, you'll need a candle, ideally a larger pillar or seven-day candle, but any kind will work. White is a good all-purpose color, but you can choose any color you like.

Place this candle in an area in need of good vibes, be it at work or home. Close your eyes and imagine a clear stream of energy descending from the sky and into the candle. The energy stream continues to pass through the bottom of the candle, deep into the earth, creating a flowing column. Place your hands around the candle and say:

This candle connects above and below,

Sending energy where it's meant to go.

Helpful energy radiates forth,

And harmful energy is fully absorbed.

When the candle is lit, good vibes will radiate into the space, while unneeded energies will be absorbed and neutralized. Be sure to extinguish the candle when you're done.

Melissa Tipton

January 29
Wednesday

1st ♓

☽ → ♈ 6:51 am

Color of the Day: White
Incense of the Day: Bay laurel

A Spell for Action

The first month of the new year is nearly over. Have you broken your resolutions or do you feel stuck in a rut? This spell will get you going in the right direction again. You'll need a candle on a heatproof surface (an orange candle is best, but anything other than black will do), matches or a lighter, and a knife.

Light the candle and pass the knife through the flame so that you cut the flame in half. Don't extinguish it though, or you'll have to start over! Do this nine times, and each time you do it, say:

I cut away what binds me

*So the fire of success may
burn inside me.*

Pinch the candle flame out between your thumb and middle finger. Your chances of being successful in your endeavors have just increased!

Charlie Rainbow Wolf

❶ January 30
Thursday

1st ♈

Color of the Day: Purple
Incense of the Day: Carnation

The Parking Space Word

I've received fan email for this spell, which I've published in various places, including earlier almanacs, so I'm repeating it this year. No matter where we live, if we drive a car, we need to park it somewhere. Whether we're at work or at the mall or at home in an urban neighborhood that has more multi-family dwellings than there are parking spaces, we need to park our car.

Speak the Parking Space Word:

ZZZZZAAAAAAZZZZZ.

Speak it loud and with great energy. It seems to work best if you plan ahead and say where you want to park. Speak the Word, therefore, when you turn a corner or enter the parking lot:

ZZZZZAAAAAZZZZZ.
Parking space at_____.

Be aware that the Word doesn't always work immediately. Sometimes you have to drive around the block or around the lot. Repeat the Word every time you turn a corner. It will work.

Barbara Ardinger

△ January 31
Friday

1st ♈

☽ v/c 10:10 am
☽ → ♉ 7:28 pm

Color of the Day: Rose
Incense of the Day: Vanilla

Dancing the Fire Within

In the midst of winter, we seek out light and heat to sustain us through these dark months. It is important to rekindle our inner flame as well. If you are able to build a fire, do so. It can be in a fireplace or outdoors. If you are in an apartment, then the flickering of a candle flame will do.

Take some time to look into the fire. See the flame and how it moves. Mimic the movements of the flame with your body. Dance and invite the fire elemental to dance with you. Let them know that you are ready to rekindle your inner flame and ask for their guidance.

Once you have finished your dance, make sure to thank the elemental for spending time with you and bid them farewell.

Charlynn Walls

February

The word *February* is based on the Latin *februa* and refers to the Roman festival of purification of the same name. This festival later became integrated with February's infamous Lupercalia. Since ancient times, February has been observed as a month of cleansing, cleaning, purification, and preparation for the warm months ahead. We see the Celtic Imbolg (Candlemas) celebrated in February to perpetuate the summoning of solar light. In many parts of the world at this time, the promise of sunlight seems bleak, even imaginary. The world around us is slowly awakening from its wintery slumber, and some semblance of excitement begins to grow in the hearts of those attuned to the seasonal tides.

Daylight hours are short in February, so this time of year can sometimes feel depressive. We must actively cultivate our inner light through regular exercise, solid sleep, meditation, yoga, ritual, studying, artwork, and planning ahead for the year. When performing magickal work this month, remember that your energy levels may be lower than usual and you must summon your own inner light to strengthen and illuminate your efforts. Do whatever it takes to stay on top of your game, keep energized, cultivate happiness, and embrace February's cleansing rebirth!

Raven Digitalis

February 1
Saturday

1st ♉
2nd Quarter 8:42 pm

Color of the Day: Indigo
Incense of the Day: Ivy

Imbolc Candle Circle

Traditionally, Imbolc begins at sundown today and continues through tomorrow. It's time to entice the sun and warmth of spring back into our lives. This was often done through the ritual lighting of candles and fires. Here is a miniature Imbolc candle ritual that can be done anywhere. Gather these materials:

- A permanent marker
- 8 multicolored birthday candles and holders (The holders are the plastic kind that can be poked into a cake.)
- A chunk of floral foam

Find a comfortable spot and spend a moment contemplating the return of warmth and sunshine, which brings with it hope, growth, and new beginnings.

Using your marker, write one intention on each birthday candle. Choose things you would like to see grow and brighten in your life as the sun returns. You can match the candle colors to your intent, such as pink for friendship or green for growth.

When you're done, place the candles in the holders and insert them into the floral foam in the shape of a circle. Light all the candles, and as they burn, feel the powerful warmth coming off them, calling back the sun, hope, springtime, and all the positive growth you'd like to see in your life. Use this time to meditate on attracting your goals until the candles burn out.

Kate Freuler

February 2
Sunday

2nd ♉

Color of the Day: Gold
Incense of the Day: Almond

Imbolc – Groundhog Day

The Quickening of the Year

By the time February arrives, many people are tired of the cold. Though springtime and warmer days are ahead, it might not feel that way. We can help things along with some sympathetic magic. For this spell, you'll need a pot, some ice cubes, a stove, and some rosemary. Rosemary is aligned with the sun and has naturally cleansing properties.

For the spell, fill a small pot halfway with ice, setting it on a cold stove. Hold either a fresh sprig or two tablespoons of dried rosemary in your hands, mentally pouring your vision of springtime warmth into the herb. Turn on the stove. As the ice begins melting, toss the herb into the pot, saying:

> *Hurry forth without delay, quicken the shifting from the cold.*

> *Winter's power shall not stay, warmth in balance shall now take hold.*

The resulting tea can be strained, sweetened, and consumed to bring some warmth within.

Michael Furie

February 3
Monday

2nd ♉

☽ v/c 6:28 am
☽ → ♊ 6:29 am

Color of the Day: Gray
Incense of the Day: Neroli

Setsubun

In Japan, today is Setsubun, which literally translates to "seasonal division." According to the lunar calendar, Setsubun marks the first day of spring. Observances of this holiday are often based in the intention to banish negativity and summon good fortune. Some households practice *mamemaki*, in which a member of the family goes outside, dons a demon mask, and knocks on the door. The other members of the family open the door and throw roasted soybeans at the "demon," chanting, *Demons out! Luck in!* until he goes away.

Try convincing someone to do this with you to purify and bless your household for the lunar cycle ahead. Otherwise, you can just open the door and throw beans out at an imagined demon for the same magical effect. Continue the traditional observance by eating one roasted soybean for every year of your life, and an additional one to bless the year ahead.

Tess Whitehurst

February 4
Tuesday

2nd ♊

Color of the Day: Red
Incense of the Day: Bayberry

A Turmeric Facial Cleanse

To invoke greater purification and clarity in your life, acquire a small amount of powdered turmeric root. In addition to being an incredibly delicious component of many curry dishes, turmeric is one of nature's best anti-inflammatories and is an excellent cleanser for the skin. This healthy plant is a member of the ginger family.

Mix the turmeric with a little warm water to create a paste. Draw sacred symbols into the paste with your fingers, and finish swirling the mix by drawing a large spiral. Envision this brilliant orange paste glowing with a cleansing light. As you do so, speak these words:

Holy root, with all your might, I cleanse myself with healing light.

Smear the paste on your face and neck, allowing it to fully dry before rinsing off. (You might want to do a patch test on your skin first to make sure you don't have an adverse reaction to the paste.) As it dries, meditate while focusing on the brew opening your chakras and providing deeply healing purification on all levels.

Raven Digitalis

February 5
Wednesday

2nd ♊

☽ v/c 9:20 am

☽ → ♋ 2:03 pm

Color of the Day: White
Incense of the Day: Honeysuckle

She Who Brings

Today is traditionally ruled by the Roman goddess Fortuna, "she who brings." In the Tarot, card X, the Wheel of Fortune, is ruled by this goddess. The illustrations on some decks show that we go both up and down as the wheel goes around.

Let's go up on Fortuna's wheel today. Let's ask her to bless us and give us good fortune. What does "good fortune" mean to you? More money? Renown? Popularity? Really great shoes? (Be careful what you ask for. It may not end up being what you envisioned.)

Pull card X out of your favorite Tarot deck and lay it in front of you. See yourself in the picture on the going-up side of the wheel. See yourself rising. See Fortuna standing at the top of the wheel, with gifts stacked all around her. Watch her select your gift. Say:

Dame Fortuna, turn your wheel for me,

Give me the best that you can see.

Barbara Ardinger

February 6
Thursday

2nd ♋

Color of the Day: Green
Incense of the Day: Apricot

A Spell to Warm the Heart

This spells aids in opening someone's heart to you so you can improve the relationship, whether it's romantic, platonic, or family.

Gather these ingredients:

- A toothpick or similar tool to carve into the candle
- A tealight candle (white, pink, or red) in a holder
- Cinnamon

Using the toothpick, draw a heart into the top of the candle, with the wick in the center of the shape. At the bottom/base of the candle, carve the initials of the person whose heart you want to open.

Light the candle, focusing on the person you wish to connect better with for approximately one minute—enough to allow the flame to melt the wax a bit. Then snuff the candle out carefully. In the warm wax, sprinkle cinnamon into the heart shape, mixing it into the wax with the toothpick. Then relight the candle and say:

With earthly spice and candlelight,
your heart shall warm to me outright.

Be sure to extinguish the candle when you're done.

Laura Tempest Zakroff

 February 7
Friday

2nd ♋

☽ v/c 10:43 am

☽ → ♌ 5:45 pm

Color of the Day: Purple
Incense of the Day: Cypress

To Draw Positive Attention to Yourself

This spell encourages recognition for your accomplishments. Your light is shining strongly today, so make the most of it! You'll need a candle in a holder and something to light it with, a hand mirror, a second mirror, and a pen (red is best) and paper.

Place the lighted candle on the hand mirror, reflective side up. Gaze at yourself in the second mirror. Look hard until you see your positive qualities. It's easy to see what you think is wrong, and the media promotes that, using presumed flaws to sell their products. They lie, so focus on all your good things and write them down.

When you're feeling strong and confident, pinch out the candle. Put the hand mirror and your list of good things in a private place, such as your underwear drawer. It should be somewhere confidential but where you will see it frequently as a reminder that you're amazing.

Charlie Rainbow Wolf

February 8
Saturday

2nd ♌

Color of the Day: Blue
Incense of the Day: Patchouli

Honoring Our Individuality

With both the sun and the moon growing in strength, it's a good time to shine a light on some of our inner mysteries.

For this spell, take a simple wooden craft store frame and place it on your altar, face up. Light a candle for both the Lord and the Lady, and let the candlelight fall on the glass in the frame. Let the patterns of light and shadow help you to ease into a trance state. Say:

*Light and dark, shadow and spark,
reveal to me my authentic self.*

*Dark and light, by my passion's
might, I am becoming my best self!*

Use paint, dried flowers, and other craft items to decorate the frame with symbols of your uniqueness. Place the frame in a prominent place on your altar to remind you to love yourself for who you are and who you believe you are meant to be.

Thuri Calafia

February 9
Sunday

2nd ♌

☽ Full Moon 2:33 am

☽ v/c 11:08 am

☽ → ♍ 6:39 pm

Color of the Day: Amber

Incense of the Day: Eucalyptus

A Full Moon Cleansing Spell

The Full Moon is an ideal time for a cleansing/clearing spell to remove bad habits, bad relationships, or other negative issues from your life. For this spell, you will need:

- A white votive candle and holder
- A small piece of plain white paper
- A black ink pen
- A clear glass bowl
- Ice

Think of a problem you wish to cleanse out of your life, then light the candle. Now write the problem on the paper. Next, fill the bowl with ice. Tear the paper into small pieces and scatter them over the ice. Extinguish the candle and allow the ice to melt.

Later, or even the next day, pour the melted ice and bits of paper onto a compost pile or the ground. Throw the candle away. Your problem will begin to diminish.

James Kambos

NOTES:

February 10
Monday

3rd ♍

Color of the Day: Ivory
Incense of the Day: Hyssop

Electrical Gratitude Spell

Edith Clarke was born on this day in 1883. She was the first woman to earn a master of science degree in electrical engineering from the Massachusetts Institute of Technology. She also worked as a "human computer" and invented the Clarke calculator, which solved equations dealing with long-distance electrical transmissions. Electricity is connected to the element of fire.

For this spell, you will need:

- 4 quarter candles in holders
- Matches
- Personal energy

Light the quarter candles. Cast a circle by cupping your hands in front of you, imagining a sphere of light. Open your hands and arms wide, imagining it encompassing your entire living space, including the attic and/or basement.

Walk through your home deosil (clockwise), placing your hands on every device that uses electricity and on every switch plate, saying:

Thank you, Edith and electricity,
for improving my quality of
life in so many ways.

Ground the energy when you've completed your circuit by placing your palms on the ground. Imagine any excess energy draining into the earth. Imagine the circle fading into the earth with it. Then extinguish the quarter candles.

This can be done seasonally or annually, as needed.

Cerridwen Iris Shea

℣ebruary 11
Tuesday

3rd ♍
☽ v/c 1:26 pm
☽ → ♎ 6:37 pm

Color of the Day: Scarlet
Incense of the Day: Cedar

Body Lovin'

Sit in a comfortable position and place your hands over your heart. Close your eyes and connect with your heartbeat, taking some time to really appreciate each beat as it circulates vital energy throughout your body. Send love to your heart. Then move your hands to different areas of your body, letting your intuition guide you. Pause at each one, sending love and giving thanks. Perhaps you thank your ribs for protecting your lungs, your hair for allowing you to feel the breeze, your feet for carrying you where you want to go.

Awareness and love-infused energy are incredibly healing, so use this time to shower your body with wellness. If you feel drawn to specific areas, ask if they have any messages for you while you infuse them with love and appreciation. This is a wonderful practice to do regularly but especially when you're feeling disconnected from or out of balance in your body.

Melissa Tipton

℣ebruary 12
Wednesday

3rd ♎

Color of the Day: Brown
Incense of the Day: Lilac

Communicating Your Needs

Communication is essential in dealing with those in our lives and also when working with deities to create change in ourselves. However, it can be difficult to clearly communicate our needs.

Today is a Wednesday, which is a good day for communication. Wear blue to increase the chances that what you are communicating will be heard and well received, and place a blue stone in your pocket. Prior to meeting with the person or group you want to communicate with, hold the stone and say:

*Hear my words and let it convey
all that I have to say.*

Finally, sit down with the individual or group you need to speak with. Take your time with the conversation and know you will be heard.

Charlynn Walls

February 13
Thursday

3rd ♎︎

☽ v/c 4:40 pm

☽ → ♏︎ 7:37 pm

Color of the Day: Turquoise
Incense of the Day: Balsam

Warm the Soul Incense

February can be the longest month of the year due to the cold and lack of sunlight. This incense is designed to warm the soul and provide some positive energy during an often bleak time of year. The incense uses things readily available in most homes, but you'll need a small piece of charcoal designed to burn incense on.

For your incense, mix and grind together any combination of the following ingredients: orange zest, clove, dried lavender, spearmint, basil, rosemary, vanilla bean, fennel, and parsley. Place on your glowing charcoal briquette and inhale the smoke. Visualize it warming you from the inside, soothing fears, worries, and any seasonal depression.

The incense may then be walked throughout your home to revitalize your living space and clear away any negative energy.

Ari & Jason Mankey

February 14
Friday

3rd ♏︎

Color of the Day: Coral
Incense of the Day: Alder

Valentine's Day

Summoning Love

The energies of love are abundant today as people all over the world celebrate Valentine's Day. We aren't celebrating romance or chocolate, but rather the gift of connection and partnership. There are many ways that love can manifest. Whether it is something that you feel is abundant in your life or something you would like more of, connecting to the spirit of love today can bring balance and empowerment to this area of life.

Sit at your altar and light a small red candle on a heatproof surface. Gaze into the flame, focus on the natural rhythm of your breath, and know that the flame embodies all love in your life, past, present, and future. Chant five times:

All life is made of matter and love.
Love is the fruit of the Goddess
and her ultimate ritual.

Allow the candle to burn down on its own, visiting it two more times to repeat the chant before it goes out.

Devin Hunter

February 15
Saturday

3rd ♏

4th Quarter 5:17 pm

☽ v/c 5:20 pm

☽ → ♐ 11:07 pm

Color of the Day: Gray
Incense of the Day: Magnolia

Life Cycles and the Magical Mobius

Winter is a good time to reflect on life's cycles. What better way to do this than with a Mobius strip?

You'll need an 8.5 x 11 sheet of paper, a scissors, and a pen. Cut a 1 x 11-inch strip from one edge of the sheet. (Set the large leftover sheet aside.) On one side of the strip, reflect on your successes or challenges over the past year, writing as little or as much (or as large!) as you wish but filling the strip with writing. Turn it over, and on the other side, write about your goals, hopes, and dreams for the coming year.

Holding the two ends of the strip, give one end a half-turn so its reverse side is visible. Tape the two ends together with the twist still present.

Sitting quietly and contemplating your successes and dreams, place your finger at any one point on the strip and follow it along, moving the strip as you go, until…what happens?

Susan Pesznecker

February 16
Sunday

4th ♐

Color of the Day: Orange
Incense of the Day: Hyacinth

Banishing Powder

To make this banishing powder, gather these ingredients:

* 1 teaspoon incense ashes
* 1 teaspoon salt
* 1 teaspoon garlic powder
* A bowl
* A pin
* Pen and paper

In the bowl, mix the first three ingredients together using the sharp end of the pin, imbuing them with the prickly, spiky energy of the needle. Imagine a black cloud surrounding the powder. Place the pin in the powder.

With the pen and paper, write down what you wish to banish, or draw a picture or symbol associated with it. Then pour the banishing powder and pin on top of it so it covers the words or drawing completely, snuffing out its power the same way dirt will stifle a fire. Leave this undisturbed until the situation is resolved. Afterward, throw everything away.

Kate Freuler

❤ February 17
Monday

4th ↗

Color of the Day: White
Incense of the Day: Narcissus

Presidents' Day

Letting Go of a Love

Unfortunately, during this month of hearts and candy, some of us must face the fact that someone we love no longer loves us. There comes a time when we must let a love go. This spell will help make this painful process easier. When you let someone you love go so that they may find happiness, you are expressing true, unselfish love.

You'll need one violet-colored candle in a holder. Light the candle. Ground and center, then say:

Once we were hand to hand
and heart to heart,

But now we must part.

I cherish the time we had together,

But I realize nothing lasts forever.

After we've said our good-byes,

I'll have peace knowing
true love never dies.

Snuff out the candle, then whisper:

My pain is now released,

May you go in peace.

Repeat this ritual until you feel a sense of calm.

James Kambos

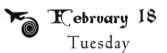

February 18
Tuesday

4th ♐

☽ v/c 4:03 am
☽ → ♑ 5:37 am
☉ → ♓ 11:57 pm

Color of the Day: Black
Incense of the Day: Cinnamon

Mercury Retrograde

Two days ago, Mercury went retrograde, and now appears to be moving backward in the sky. In recent years, Mercury retrograde periods have accumulated an impressive load of superstitions, such as "don't sign contracts" and "don't make major purchases." In fact, Mercury is the planet of communication, commerce, and travel, and when Mercury is retrograde, it is simply a time to look more closely at these areas in order to reassess, reformulate, revise, and renew.

Today, cleanse a light-colored agate in running water, sunlight, and/or sage smoke. Hold it in your right hand and empower it with the intention to approach this time with a steady mind and a positive attitude. Call on the god Mercury to align you with divine timing and to help you see the ways you can leverage this energy for clarity, harmony, abundance, and success. Keep the agate with you until Mercury goes direct on March 9.

Tess Whitehurst

February 19
Wednesday

4th ♑

Color of the Day: Yellow
Incense of the Day: Marjoram

The Mutable Water

Shortly before the day begins, the sun moves into the zodiac sign of Pisces, the last of the twelve signs. Pisces is considered a "mutable" water sign, which means that it is adaptable, and it is ruled by Neptune, the planet of dreams and imagination. We can take a cue from the energy shift today and seek assistance with our creative projects.

Filling a glass with pure, cold water, you can imprint the desire for creative inspiration into the water and then drink it to absorb its energy. This simple action will help empower your imagination and all your artistic endeavors.

Michael Furie

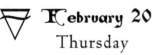

▽ **February 20**
Thursday

4th ♑

☽ v/c 9:18 am

☽ → ♒ 2:42 pm

Color of the Day: Purple
Incense of the Day: Mulberry

Tree Offering Grounding Spell

To ground yourself to Mother Nature, especially if you've been feeling flighty or spacey lately, pluck a strand of your hair. (If you're bald, like me, you can pluck it from another part of your body.) Venture outside and spend some time reflecting on the trees around you. See if any tree in particular seems to call out to you, and make your way to its trunk.

Lean against the tree and inhale the fresh oxygen it's giving off. Offer the tree your breath. When you're ready, very carefully tie the strand of hair to one of its branches. While doing this, envision roots sprouting from the soles of your feet, bringing the nourishing essence of the Mighty Mother (this energy is also called Shakti) up into your body.

Declare:

*I am connected, I am grounded,
for I am a child of nature and
the teachings of the earth!*

Don't forget to practice recycling, sustainable eating, earth-conscious purchasing, and other positive Pagan acts to give back to our Great Mother.

Raven Digitalis

 **February 21**
Friday

4th ♒
☽ v/c 11:08 pm

Color of the Day: Pink
Incense of the Day: Thyme

Banishing Bad Habits Spell

For each bad habit you wish to banish, take a small piece of paper. Write words or phrases that describe the bad habit and the ways in which it's hurting you. (For example, you might write "soda pop" and all of its health implications, or "negative thinking" and all of its energetic consequences.)

Cast a protective circle, then invite and safely light a black candle for your most powerful protective deity. Tell your deity that you wish to be free of this habit and why. Chant:

By (name of deity) and me,
I set myself free!

(Bad habit) be gone!

Follow up by keeping that energy away from yourself. Repeat the chant whenever you feel drawn to return to the bad habit.

Thuri Calafia

 **February 22**
Saturday

4th ♒

Color of the Day: Black
Incense of the Day: Pine

Thought on the Wind Spell

The World Association of Girl Guides and Girl Scouts celebrates February 22 as World Thinking Day, which focuses on global connectivity and personal impact. Even if you're not part of the organization, take a moment to reflect on how we are all interconnected and the impact you can have on others. What is one thing that you excel at that you wish to share more of with the world? How can that ability impact others positively?

Light your favorite incense in a transportable container that you can hold. As you contemplate, watch how the smoke filters into the air around you, dispersing everywhere. When the answer comes to you, take the incense and circle the room you are in three times clockwise, saying:

Element of air, carry my thoughts on
your winds to all corners of the earth.
May I be able to give others support
the way air guides the sails of ships.

Laura Tempest Zakroff

February 23
Sunday

4th ♒

☽ → ♓ 1:37 am

New Moon 10:32 am

Color of the Day: Yellow
Incense of the Day: Marigold

Tween the Seasons
Beat the Blues Spell

By the end of February, it can feel like winter will last forever. This late-month new moon is a great time to do a spell to lift your spirits.

Gather these supplies:

- Fabric and objects that make you happy
- Yellow candles (2 or as many as you want) in holders
- The Sun tarot card
- Citrus oil in a burner or citrus incense
- Your favorite beverage
- Your favorite dessert
- Brightly colored plates and cups

Decorate your space with fabric and objects that make you happy in colors that brighten your mood. Light the candles, placing the Sun tarot card in front of them. Scent the room with citrus.

Enjoy eating and drinking in this cheerful space, and know that the season will soon change and wonderful things are possible. Burn the candles a few minutes every day until they are finished.

Cerridwen Iris Shea

February 24
Monday

1st ♓

Color of the Day: Silver
Incense of the Day: Lily

Dream Pillow

During the long winter months is a time to dream. The long nights tend to help promote dreaming as we snuggle under our covers for warmth.

A dream pillow can aid you in the pursuit of dreams that will provide insight into your daily life. You can create one out of fabric and fill it, or you can purchase a small pillow. You can stuff the pillow with dried peppermint, yarrow, or cedar. If you have access to essential oils, they can be substituted and used to scent the pillow.

Once you have your pillow prepared, simply fall asleep on it as you think about the question you need to have answered. The dream pillow will also help you hold onto the dream longer once you awaken.

Charlynn Walls

NOTES:

February 25
Tuesday

1st ♓

☽ v/c 9:12 am

☽ → ♈ 1:47 pm

Color of the Day: Maroon
Incense of the Day: Ylang-ylang

Mardi Gras (Fat Tuesday)

Dionysus Spell for Excess and Abundance

Fat Tuesday is the peak of Mardi Gras season, a time of excess and abundance. In the ancient world, Dionysus was often associated with excess, so he's the perfect deity to celebrate with today.

For this spell, call up some friends and either prepare an indulgent meal or plan a visit to your favorite restaurant. Once the meal has been served and everyone is comfortable eating and drinking, say this toast to Dionysus:

*What we have shared together
will come back threefold,*

*As the laws of magick have
promised and foretold!*

*Let there be joy, food, and
abundance in this place.*

*This we ask by your power
and your grace!*

So mote it be!

Make sure to fix a plate (and a drink!) for Dionysus, and then present this to him as an offering at the end of your meal.

Ari & Jason Mankey

February 26
Wednesday

1st ♈

Color of the Day: Topaz
Incense of the Day: Lavender

Ash Wednesday

Honoring the Ancestors

Ash Wednesday reminds Christians that everything returns to dust. To me, this day also speaks of the ancestors, and it reminds me to pay respect.

To set up an ancestor altar, find a likely spot in your home and place an altar cloth there if desired. Add photographs, tchotchke, and other items that remind you of your dearly departed. Depending on your magical traditions, you may also wish to add items related to a deity or path. I like to include representations of the four elements. Consider adding candles or a small string of white or colored lights.

Work with the altar on your ancestors' birthdays or other dates of importance. (I always include Samhain.) Leave offerings of food or drink, lighting the candles as you do so. Offer a small prayer:

To the Shining Ones, always with me, may I be worthy, may we never truly part. What is remembered never dies.

Susan Pesznecker

▽ **February 27**
Thursday

1st ♈

☽ v/c 10:25 pm

Color of the Day: White
Incense of the Day: Clove

Dreamy Face Steam

Use this face steam before bed to receive dream insights on a desired question. You'll need two tablespoons dried lavender, a heat-proof bowl, boiling water, and a towel.

Add the lavender to the bowl, then pour the boiling water over the herbs. Check to make sure the steam isn't too hot. Put your face over the bowl, using the towel to create a tent, trapping the steam. Focus on your question and say:

I call upon the powers of water and lavender, and I open to receive insights to my question in my dreams tonight.

Water is symbolic of the intuition and the unconscious, and as it transforms into steam, it transitions into the air realm of the conscious mind. Thus, performing this steam before bed aids in bridging the gap between the unconscious and conscious realms, making it easier to translate the messages of your dreams into a format that the waking mind can understand. Sweet dreams!

Melissa Tipton

▽ **February 28**
Friday

1st ♈

☽ → ♉ 2:30 am

Color of the Day: Rose
Incense of the Day: Orchid

Earthen Shield for Empaths and Sensitives

The waxing moon has just moved into Taurus, bringing with it energies that will stir the inner worlds and enhance our imagination as well as our psychic centers. The sun is also in Pisces, so all matters related to the psychic and unseen are likely to be at the forefront of our senses. Today, you are likely to be extra-sensitive, and you might find it difficult to ground your empathic abilities. Cast this spell to invoke the element of earth to wrap around you and act as a psychic shield and to help ground extra energy.

Using your right foot, draw an X on the ground, then stomp with your left foot on the center of the X. As you do this, say:

An earthen shield to disrupt the field,
a Gaian blessing for me to wield!

Visualize a large stone growing from the X, encasing you in an impermeable psychic shield.

Devin Hunter

🏅 **February 29**
Saturday

1st ♉

Color of the Day: Brown
Incense of the Day: Ivy

To Ensure Long-Term Success

Today's magic only comes around every four years, and brings with it a chance to set a long-term plan in motion. The spell enhances your chances of accomplishment. You'll need a candle in a holder, something to light it with, an unused notebook, and a pen.

Light the candle and gaze into the flame. Imagine the flame bringing light and life to your ambitions. Form a plan of action to make this a reality. Take your time with this, and really see it, step by step. Put today's date on the first page of the notebook, and write down all your thoughts.

Pinch out the flame, and keep the candle and the notebook in a private place. Whenever you find your determination wobbling, light the candle, grab the notebook, and write out your thoughts. Let the magic that you started tonight carry you forward to success.

Charlie Rainbow Wolf

March

March is upon us! March is a month of unpredictable weather. Will the weather spirits decide to bring us a last hurrah of winter in the form of a blustery snowstorm or instead bring us signs of spring's beginning in the form of budding trees and perhaps rain showers sprinkled with mild, sunny days? There really is no telling! However, for those of us who follow the Wheel of the Year, the spring equinox is a time of new beginnings, regardless of the weather.

Rituals of spring and new beginnings will take place around the globe this month. Druids still gather at Stonehenge to welcome the rising sun on the morning of the equinox. March also is the time to celebrate the festival of Holi, popular in India and Nepal. People engage in paint fights, covering each other in festive splatters of vibrant color, welcoming the arrival of spring and all its vibrancy.

In March, however you choose to celebrate, work the magick of new beginnings!

Blake Octavian Blair

March 1
Sunday

1st ♉

☽ v/c 10:52 am

☽ → ♊ 2:21 pm

Color of the Day: Yellow
Incense of the Day: Frankincense

Clear Communication Spell

Oftentimes when we have miscommunications with the people in our lives, we find it easy to place the blame wholly on them. However, we know in our hearts that it takes two people to create conflict and it takes two people to resolve conflict.

For this spell, take a small blade or wooden pick and inscribe a white pillar candle with words and symbols representing what you want the other person to do to help ease the communication difficulty. On a second white pillar candle, inscribe words and symbols representing what *you* need to do. (Hint: When you're done, *your* candle should be the one with the most carvings!)

Set the candles about a foot apart, light them safely, and say:

May the air be sweet between us,
may our minds be filled with light.

May we each bring all the best
that we have, no matter who's
wrong or who's right!

Repeat every night until the full moon, moving the candles closer each time. Follow up with a heartfelt conversation.

Thuri Calafia

March 2
Monday

1st ♊

2nd Quarter 2:57 pm

Color of the Day: Ivory
Incense of the Day: Clary sage

honoring Mars Ritual

March is named in honor of the Roman god Mars. He is the god of war, but originally he was the god of agriculture and abundance. This ritual honors his agricultural aspect and helps us to be mindful of where our food comes from. You'll need four small candles in various colors of your choice, one for each season. You'll also need a small saucer of soil and one penny.

Place the saucer of soil on your altar, and arrange the candles around the saucer in holders. Light them, then say:

Mars, god of crops and the fields,

God of the land and all that it yields,

Bless the farmers as they toil,

Bless the earth and renew the soil.

As an offering, place the penny into the soil. Extinguish the candles. (They may be used again for magic.) End by scattering the soil on the ground outside and pressing the penny into the earth.

James Kambos

March 3
Tuesday

2nd ♊

☽ v/c 9:20 pm

☽ → ♋ 11:25 pm

Color of the Day: Black
Incense of the Day: Basil

Ditch Dolls

Today is Hinamatsuri, the Japanese doll festival. Dolls representing the Heian court are displayed on a red-carpeted platform. Participants also make dolls out of paper or straw and sail them down a river to remove impurities.

For a modern Western twist on this, you will need:

• A large leaf or other compostable, recyclable material for each attribute you wish to release

• Scissors

• Water

Cut each leaf into a doll-like shape. Take your leaves to a moving body of water. Drop each leaf into the water, saying:

(Attribute), flow out of my life, making room for something better.

Or rip each leaf into tiny pieces as you name and release the attribute, then wash the pieces down the drain in your sink.

When you have ditched all your dolls, give thanks, turn, and walk away without looking back.

You have taken literal steps to release what no longer works for you!

Cerridwen Iris Shea

March 4
Wednesday

2nd ♋

Color of the Day: Brown
Incense of the Day: Bay laurel

What Is in a Name?

Today is Discover What Your Name Means Day! Some magickal practitioners use their given name, and others have taken on a different moniker for spiritual use. No matter what name you use, take some time to discover what it means to you and develop a sigil that represents yourself for use in spells and rituals.

Sit in a quiet place and close your eyes. Say out loud the name you use. What images does it bring to mind? What words do you associate with it: kind, loving, honorable? Make a mental note of the images and words that spring forth as you say your name.

Once you are confident that you are finished, take out a sheet of paper and a pen. Write down or sketch what you visualized. Are there any commonalities in the structure of the words or drawings? Take those common pieces and place them together in an image that is unique to you!

Charlynn Walls

 ## March 5
Thursday

2nd ♋

Color of the Day: Purple
Incense of the Day: Carnation

Spring Clearing

Many of us engage in the annual ritual known as spring cleaning. Add a little zing to your cleaning with magical techniques that go beyond soap and water.

Working with a new broom, move deosil (sunwise) through your home and through each room, sweeping out both dust (bury this outdoors) and spiritual detritus.

Bind together stems of lavender, rosemary, and/or hyssop. Dissolve a bit of sea salt in spring water. Dip your stem "wand" into the water and asperge (sprinkle) your rooms for magical cleansing.

Anoint candles with olive or frankincense oil and leave them to burn safely in each cleansed room. If you prefer, smudge the room with sage or juniper (but beware, your smoke alarm might go off!).

Hang small bells in each room and let the moving air catch them. Say:

Cleansing now, for seasons' turn,

Herbals pure and candles burn.

Wand of water, small bells ring,

Rising spirits soon to sing!

Susan Pesznecker

March 6
Friday

2nd ♋

☽ v/c 2:11 am

☽ → ♌ 4:27 am

Color of the Day: White
Incense of the Day: Rose

Anxiety/Stress Relief Incense

Anxiety and stress can get the best of anyone, but when the moon is in Leo like it is now, these emotions can become overwhelming. Blend this special incense and burn it over charcoal as often as you need to relieve the pressures of anxiety and stress or to help balance the energies of the inner and outer worlds.

Combine and grind together the following ingredients:

- 1 gram amber resin
- 1 gram black copal
- ⅓ ounce sweetgrass

As you mix the ingredients together, chant:

Soothe and soften, comfort and console.

Amber, copal, and sweetgrass, make me whole.

Roll the mixture into small balls the size of the nail of your index finger, then safely burn.

Devin Hunter

March 7
Saturday

2nd ♌

Color of the Day: Black
Incense of the Day: Sandalwood

The Mother of Us All

Unlike some people who follow the standard-brand religions, we Pagans know that our Mother Planet is alive and conscious. She is the mother of us all, from water and rocks to trees, grass, and gardens to microbes, to cockroaches, mice and rats, and elephants, to pigeons and ravens, and to every human being of any gender or skin color. Celebrate your connection to our Mother Planet today.

First, do some recycling. What do you have that you no longer use but someone else could use? What does not need to go into a landfill? Second, volunteer where volunteers are truly needed. What sisters or brothers can you help? Third, gather your circle or community for a ritual of gratitude that we live on a generous planet. Promise to work for her good health.

Mother Planet, bless your children, bless us all,

Bless and keep us, summer, winter, spring, and fall.

Barbara Ardinger

March 8
Sunday

2nd ♌

☽ v/c 4:12 am

☽ → ♍ 6:47 am

Color of the Day: Amber
Incense of the Day: Juniper

Daylight Saving Time
begins at 2:00 a.m.

Empathy within the Family

Our lives with our families aren't always an easy ride. Many ancient cultures understood that life lessons and karmic bonds are interwoven with individuals who either are our family by birth or become our family during life's journey.

To help encourage positive thoughts, speech, and actions within the family, construct this charm bag—or multiple bags, if you wish!

Obtain a sachet bag and add to it any combination of peppermint, lavender, sage, cinnamon, and/or rosemary, as well as a small piece of amethyst crystal. Focus strongly on the bag when you are in sacred space, repeating the words *Peace and joy and love to all* until you can palpably feel the bag as fully enchanted.

The bag should be left in a location that you and your family frequent. Even if you feel the need to hide the charm where no one can find it, the important thing is that you know its magick is present and ever weaving onward in a positive direction.

Raven Digitalis

March 9
Monday

2nd ♏

🌕 Full Moon 1:48 pm

Color of the Day: Lavender
Incense of the Day: Neroli

Full Moon Prosperity Spell

Using a small mirror, reflect the light of the full moon into a small piece of aventurine (a type of green crystal) or a coin such as a nickel or a dime. This can be done either outside or near a window inside. As the moonlight is reflected into your stone or coin, imagine the object you are using absorbing the energy of the moon.

When you are done, keep your stone or coin on your person, either in a pocket or in your purse. It will attract money and prosperity to you. If its power starts to drain, simply add more to it on the next full moon night.

If you have a big piece of aventurine, you can charge it with the power of the moon using this technique and then transfer that energy to smaller items as needed. It's like having a giant moon battery!

Ari & Jason Mankey

March 10
Tuesday

3rd ♏

☽ v/c 4:32 am

☽ → ♎ 6:03 am

Color of the Day: Red
Incense of the Day: Geranium

Purim (begins at
sundown on March 9)

Zesty Purification Candle

This candle is an easy and effective means of clearing out any astral buildup or bad vibes in your environment. Items needed:

- ½ cup safflower oil
- 1 bay leaf
- ½ teaspoon each lemon, lime and grapefruit zest
- 1 white candle

Combine the oil with the bay leaf and the citrus zests in a small pot and warm them over low heat on the stove. Once you can smell the oil in the air, remove from heat and allow it to cool.

Anoint the candle with the oil and place it in a sturdy holder. Then light it, carrying it from room to room so that its power is fully released.

Michael Furie

March 11
Wednesday

3rd ♎

Color of the Day: Yellow
Incense of the Day: Lilac

Apple Divination

March 11 is Johnny Appleseed Day, which celebrates the life of a real person: John Chapman. Reputed to be a kind man, he was a leader in conservation and is responsible for introducing apple trees to many areas of the United States.

The apple has a long history of being used in Witchcraft. If you cut an apple in half horizontally (not through the stem), you will often find that the seeds form a pentagram.

If you wish to know how a ritual or spell will go, place an apple on your altar before you start. After you finish the working, slice the apple in half and study what you find. If it looks pleasing, eat one half and leave the other half as an offering outside. If the results are less than favorable, instead of consuming your half, bury it in the earth or compost.

Laura Tempest Zakroff

March 12
Thursday

3rd ♎

☽ v/c 4:12 am
☽ → ♏ 5:28 am

Color of the Day: White
Incense of the Day: Jasmine

A Spell for Balance

We're coming down off the full moon energy, and this spell will help you keep things in balance. It focuses on restoring harmony in all areas of your life, from finances to relationships—even your relationship with yourself. You'll need an amethyst or other purple stone, a white candle on a heatproof surface, and something to light the candle with.

Light the candle and pick up the stone. Focus on the stone drawing out whatever is causing the imbalance in your life so the space can be filled with harmony and stability. When you feel yourself coming back to your center, carefully pass the stone through the candle flame and say:

I pass the crystal through the light,

For peace and calm and all that's right.

Pinch out the flame and put the stone somewhere private but where you'll see it often. This spell can be repeated at any time.

Charlie Rainbow Wolf

March 13
Friday

3rd ♏

Color of the Day: Rose
Incense of the Day: Yarrow

Wish You Were here

Use this spell if you want to travel to a particular place and your travel budget needs a little boost. First, buy or make a postcard of your desired destination. On the reverse, write a message from your future self (who is already at the destination) and share at least one reason why the trip is a wonderful experience. End with this:

I can't wait to see you here!

Next, hold the postcard in both hands and imagine yourself at this destination, tapping into how you feel while you're there. Then say:

All details of my trip to (name of place) are unfolding in a manner that is correct and for the highest good.

Stamp the card and mail it to yourself. When it arrives, once again tap into the feeling and excitement of being there, and place the postcard someplace where you'll see it every day. Pay attention to any intuitive guidance pointing you toward choices and opportunities that support your spell's unfolding.

Melissa Tipton

March 14
Saturday

3rd ♏

☽ v/c 6:06 am
☽ → ♐ 7:09 am

Color of the Day: Blue
Incense of the Day: Sage

Pi Day

It's Pi Day, a celebration of the mathematical constant that is (among other things) the ratio of any circle's circumference to its diameter. Since pi begins with 3.14 (hence the date), it is an irrational number that continues infinitely after the decimal. In addition to eluding accurate definition by being unending, pi is a transcendental number: it is impossible to express using rational numbers and impossible to construct geometrically with programs or tools. Pi was of vital importance to the mathematical and architectural studies of a number of ancient cultures around the world, including those of Greece and Egypt.

Today, bake or purchase a delicious pie. (In addition to being a pun on *pi*, a pie is a circle and therefore an actual representation of pi.) Light a candle and enjoy the pie with one or more friends as you quietly contemplate the transcendent and infinite nature of the cosmos and the entire physical world.

Tess Whitehurst

March 15
Sunday

3rd ♐

Color of the Day: Orange
Incense of the Day: Eucalyptus

Renew Your Spirit Spell

Spring is near. Though frost is still in the ground in many places, March is a good time to renew your spirit. Use this spell to ready yourself for spring or to rise to meet any challenge. You'll need a small dish of garden or potting soil, one green candle, and one light blue candle.

Place the dish of soil in the center of your altar. Set a candle in a holder on each side of the dish, but don't light them yet. Sit before the altar and say:

In the zodiac, the fishes and
the ram rule Father Sky.

Beneath the earth, the
Goddess begins to stir.

Father Sky and Mother Earth,
renew my spirit, let it fly.

Now light the candles. Visualize your spirit soaring as you accomplish your goals. End by sprinkling the soil around a tree. Extinguish the candles and use them for other nature magic spells.

James Kambos

NOTES:

March 16
Monday

3rd ♐

☽ v/c 5:34 am

4th Quarter 5:34 am

☽ → ♑ 12:25 pm

Color of the Day: Gray

Incense of the Day: Rosemary

Banishing Lack Spell

For this spell, you'll need a black candle in a holder, burnable copies of your bills, and a heatproof container in which to burn them, such as a small cauldron or a plant pot plate painted black.

Find a safe place to do this sacred burning, then cast a circle around you and invite your chosen guardians and gods in your usual way. Take a moment to let your imagination wander to all the worst-case scenarios that have been playing in your head lately. Then take a small blade or wooden pick and inscribe the candle with symbols and words representing those fears. Let the energy build by reviewing the bills you feel especially fearful about, then say:

> As the moon wanes, so let poverty
> and lack wane. Blessed Lord and
> Lady, take these burdens from me.

Take the bills, one at a time, and as you say these words, light each bill in turn in the candle flame, then quickly place them into the container you brought and watch them burn. As each bill burns, visualize it getting paid in full and on time. After all the bills have burned, take some time and gaze at the candle flame and allow yourself to relax and open to the peace of debt relief.

Be sure to follow up with energies conducive to getting your bills paid, such as taking the offer of working overtime or reining in your spending. You might also choose to buy a lottery ticket!

Thuri Calafia

March 17
Tuesday

4♄ ♑

Color of the Day: Maroon
Incense of the Day: Cedar

Saint Patrick's Day

Snakes of Transformation Spell

Rather than celebrate Saint Patrick today, let's celebrate snakes.

Snakes are symbols of transformation. Medusa, the snake-haired goddess who could turn men to stone with a glance, aids dramatic change. The ribbons in this spell symbolize snakes. As they twist in the wind, they represent the intellect and the element of air—new ideas to manifest change.

Gather these supplies:

- Ribbons in colors corresponding to your desired changes

- A marker in a color that contrasts with the ribbons

- A place to hang the ribbons where air will move them (a curtain rod, tree branch, etc.)

Using the marker, write one desired change on each ribbon. Tie the ribbons to the curtain rod or tree branch (or whatever you choose to use). Say:

Medusa, please aid me in being the transformation I see in my life, taking action rather than going along to get along. Let the snakes of transformation twist in the winds of change. So mote it be.

As each change initiates, remove the ribbon and continue the work.

Cerridwen Iris Shea

March 18
Wednesday

4th ♑

☽ v/c 8:48 pm

☽ → ♒ 9:16 pm

Color of the Day: Topaz
Incense of the Day: Marjoram

Magical Fertilizer

Did you know that a great way to help your indoor potted plants grow is by adding crushed eggshells to the soil? Just rinse the shells thoroughly, run them through a blender, and then sprinkle them into the dirt. You can turn this into a magickal process simply by adding a little food coloring and visualization to the blender as well. Put a drop of the following colors in your eggshell fertilizer to grow some magick along with your plants:

- *Pink:* Love and friendship

- *Green:* Prosperity

- *Blue:* Protection

- *Purple:* Spirituality

- *Brown:* Stability

- *Orange:* Success

- *Yellow:* Communication

Visualize your goal as you sprinkle the shells into your plants. As your greenery grows, your wishes will manifest. (Don't do this more than once a year or it may upset the pH balance of the soil.)

Kate Freuler

March 19
Thursday

4th ♒

☉ → ♈ 11:50 pm

Color of the Day: Green
Incense of the Day: Apricot

Spring Equinox – Ostara

Equinox New Beginnings Spell

Blessed equinox, witches! Cast this spell before midnight and use the energy of the day to bring blessings to a new beginning. You will need:

- A crayon
- 1 fresh egg
- Flower seeds of any kind

With a crayon, draw an image on the egg that symbolizes the new beginning you seek, such as a picture of a house for a new home, a heart for new love, etc. Dig a hole a few inches into the ground and hold the flower seeds in both hands. Gently blow over them to empower them and say:

A new beginning from growing seeds, bringing balance, focus, change, and disciplined deeds!

Then place the seeds in the hole. Crack the egg over the seeds, put the shells in the hole, then cover with soil as you say:

So must this be, for the good of all, but mostly for me!

As spring emerges and your flowers bloom, so too will your fresh start.

Devin Hunter

March 20
Friday

4th ♒

☽ v/c 5:00 am

Color of the Day: Purple
Incense of the Day: Vanilla

Mercury Spell for Safe Travels

Traveling is part of life. Some of us commute to work each day. Sometimes the travel is longer for business, and at other times we travel for pleasure. No matter why you or a loved one are traveling, you can do this quick spell for safe travels.

Mercury, a Roman deity who aided travelers, can speed travel and provide safe passage. Take a piece of paper and cut out a small wing or draw one if you do not have ready access to scissors. Write down where you will be traveling from and where you will be traveling to. Call to Mercury, saying:

From here to there and back,
please ensure a safe journey.

Now place this item in your travel bag before the start of the trip.

Charlynn Walls

March 21
Saturday

4th ♒

☽ → ♓ 8:33 am

Color of the Day: Indigo
Incense of the Day: Rue

Plant Your Garden

In his novel *Candide, or Optimism,* the French author Voltaire sends his hero through all kinds of disasters. Candide's teacher, Dr. Pangloss, keeps telling him it's all for the best in this best of all possible worlds. That wasn't true in 1756, when the novel was published, nor is it true today. What can we do to help make this struggling planet a better world for all men and women? What Candide eventually learns is that "when man was first placed in the Garden of Eden, he was put there…that he might cultivate it." What can we cultivate?

Gather with your circle or community and plant a garden of flowers and veggies. Then plant a metaphorical garden that will bloom with friendship, good works, and realistic optimism. Join hands and declare this blessing:

We're here to plant our garden,

Helping flowers grow,

Extraordinary blossoms

Only friendship can bestow.

So mote it be!

Barbara Ardinger

March 22
Sunday

4th ♓

Color of the Day: Gold
Incense of the Day: Almond

Dry Floor Wash Cleansing

Have a room that needs a bit of an energy cleansing? Mix up this dry floor wash and grab your broom!
  Gather these ingredients:

- 3 tablespoons sea salt
- ½ cup each of dried rosemary, vervain, and sage
- A jar

Mix the ingredients together in the jar, then sprinkle it on the floor of the room in a counterclockwise motion. Start in the north and sprinkle just enough to make it around the room in a spiral three times. Allow the mixture to sit for fifteen minutes.

Next, take up your broom and, continuing in the same direction, sweep up the mixture, for as long as it takes. Once you're satisfied that you have swept it all up, sweep the room one more time, this time in a clockwise direction.

If possible, dispose of your sweepings in a small fire.

Laura Tempest Zakroff

March 23
Monday

4th ♓
☽ v/c 10:51 am
☽ → ♈ 8:58 pm

Color of the Day: Silver
Incense of the Day: Hyssop

Spring Cleaning Spell

Spring is a great time for getting bad energy out of your home. This is an easy way to rid your house of unwanted energies.

Start by placing a small crystal you are comfortable parting with near a door in your home. Then take a bowl of salted water, and using your fingers, sprinkle the water/salt mixture around your entire house, being sure to get the mixture behind doors, in corners, and around windowpanes. The salted water will kick up any negative energy in your home, which you can then sweep into your crystal using a besom or an ordinary broom. If there was a lot of negativity in your home, the crystal may end up being hot to the touch. If this is the case, we suggest picking it up with an oven mitt and burying it outdoors.

Follow this up by smudging your home with sage to fill it with positive energy.

Ari & Jason Mankey

March 24
Tuesday

4th ♈

New Moon 5:28 am

Color of the Day: Gray
Incense of the Day: Ginger

Feel Into Your Truth

The initial darkness of the new moon suggests that beginnings occur in the absence of seeing. This is the energy of embarking on a path even when we're unsure where it will take us; lacking sight, we must rely on feeling. This is a wonderful balance to the tendency to overthink our way through life.

When the moon is invisible or barely visible in the night sky, perform this exercise with eyes closed to ignite your feeling sense and unite it with your intellect, supercharging your ability to make clear decisions.

Tune into your body, scanning slowly from head to toe, noticing any sensations without judging or labeling them. Breathe for a few rounds, connecting with this heightened awareness of felt sense in your body. Shift your attention to your mind, and imagine a mind light expanding into every pocket of your body, uniting feeling and thought. Bring to mind a question, and allow both modes of knowing to forge an intuitive-intellectual response.

Melissa Tipton

 March 25
Wednesday

1st ♈

Color of the Day: White
Incense of the Day: Honeysuckle

Woven Protection for the Notorious

Weave a simple spell for someone you wish to protect, whether near or far.

Start with a 6-inch square of paper, then cut it into six 6 x 1-inch strips. Write the name of the person you wish to protect on both sides of the first strip. Write "WATER" and "EARTH" on both sides of strips two and three; dip them in salt water and allow to dry. Write "AIR" and "FIRE" on both sides of strips four and five; safely pass them through the smoke above a burning candle. Customize the sixth strip with your choice of colors, runes, powdered herbs, names of deities, or any other protection you wish the strip to hold.

Weave the six strips together, adding dots of glue to hold them tight. Set it on your altar; each time you pass by, say:

Earth and air, fire and water, warp and weft, you're safe and blessed!

Susan Pesznecker

March 26
Thursday

1st ♈

☽ v/c 3:16 am

☽ → ♉ 9:37 am

Color of the Day: Turquoise
Incense of the Day: Myrrh

Protection Spell Jar

Here is how to make a powerful protection spell jar. Most of the ingredients can be found at the supermarket. Nettle and mullein may be more difficult to obtain, but most health food stores have them.

- 1 tablespoon nettle
- 1 tablespoon mint
- 1 tablespoon mullein
- 1 tablespoon oregano
- 1 small Mason jar (1 or 2-cup size)
- Soy (vegetable) oil

Each of the ingredients is attuned to protection. Combine the herbs and put them in the jar, then pour in enough oil to fill it to the top. Before sealing the jar, empower it by holding your hands over it, sending protection energy into the jar. Put the lid on tightly and place the jar where you will see it often. Whenever you feel in need of some extra protection, lightly shake the jar like a snow globe to "excite" the magic.

Michael Furie

March 27
Friday

1st ♉

Color of the Day: Coral
Incense of the Day: Mint

A Spell to Increase Your Personal Power

This spell might not make you rich or famous, but it will help you to see your worth so you can reach your greatest level of happiness and success. You'll need a ring of some sort, one that fits comfortably on your middle finger but that you don't wear daily.

Go outside at sundown and place the ring on the middle finger of your non-dominant hand. As you do, say:

I wear this ring to awaken my potential.

By the grace of the earth and the light of the sky,

I am empowered and alive!

Sleep wearing the ring, then place it under your pillow during the day. Wear the ring while sleeping for the next eleven nights, then put it in a safe place. Whenever you want to reactivate the spell, simply wear the ring while you sleep and place it under your pillow the following day.

Charlie Rainbow Wolf

March 28
Saturday

1st ♉

☽ v/c 7:05 pm

☽ → ♊ 9:38 pm

Color of the Day: Gray
Incense of the Day: Magnolia

Justice Thread Spell

This spell will help to bring justice to any situation where it is needed. You will need these items:

- White thread, at least 12 inches long
- Black thread, at least 12 inches long

Hold the white thread in your left hand and the black thread in your right. Join them together (into a double thread) and say:

May shadow and light combine to illuminate the way for justice.

Then make a central knot in the threads, saying:

By this first knot be, justice shall see.

Next, make a knot on the left side, saying:

By knot of two, justice be true.

Lastly, tie the third knot on the right side to even it out, saying:

By knot of three, so mote it be.

Carry the double thread with you or give it to a person who needs it.

Laura Tempest Zakroff

March 29
Sunday

1st ♊

Color of the Day: Amber
Incense of the Day: Heliotrope

Maiden, Mother, Crone: Loving Guides

We all deserve to feel love within ourselves and be able to receive it just as fully. Purchase (or grow) three roses or similarly beautiful flowers. When the flowers are at their peak of beauty, use natural twine (such as jute or cotton) to tie them together with three knots at nighttime, when the waxing moon rides high.

When tying the first knot, say:

To the mighty Maiden: Great Goddess in her youthful form, I offer these flowers to invoke compassion in my heart, both within myself and all around me.

Tie the second knot, saying:

To the mighty Mother: Great Goddess in her life-giving form, I offer these flowers to invoke strength and resilience, that I am born of love and will live love in this life.

Tie the third knot and declare:

To the mighty Crone: Great Goddess in her wizened form, I offer these flowers to invoke the wisdom of cosmic love and bliss, that I ever radiate pure love, inside and out.

Put the flowers in a natural place where you can feel the emerging signs of spring.

Raven Digitalis

March 30
Monday

1st ♈ ♊

☽ v/c 11:10 am

Color of the Day: White
Incense of the Day: Lily

National Doctors' Day

Regardless of how well we take care of our own health, almost all of us find ourselves needing to visit a doctor from time to time. Honoring doctors and thinking positive thoughts about them helps ensure that we'll always find a good doctor when we need one and that our doctors will always treat us with a great deal of fairness, attention, and respect.

Today, safely light a white candle and invoke Archangel Raphael, the divine healer angel. Take a moment to give thanks for all the wise, knowledgeable, and compassionate doctors of the world. Ask Raphael to bless them and infuse them with divine knowledge and the divine power to heal. Imagine them being filled and surrounded with white light. If you'd like, finish by donating any amount of your choice to the Red Cross, Doctors Without Borders, or another charity that offers professional medical care to those in need.

Tess Whitehurst

 ## March 31
Tuesday

1st ♈ ♊

☽ → ♋ 7:43 am

Color of the Day: Scarlet
Incense of the Day: Geranium

Lucky Steps

Want luck to follow you everywhere you go? Make the insoles of your shoes into potent luck-attracting amulets that no one will know about but you.

You can purchase inexpensive shoe insoles, usually meant for deodorizing footwear, in most department stores.

Using a green marker, draw a picture of a four-leaf clover on the insole. It's best to draw this on the side that will be against the sole of the shoe and not your foot in order to keep green marker from bleeding onto your socks. Add a drop of peppermint oil to the clover and imagine yourself surrounded by a lucky gold or green glow.

Place these in your shoes and go about your business knowing that lucky energy is right on your heels.

Kate Freuler

April

This month we move from dark to light, from cold to warm, from brown to green. April is a magical month that starts with April Fools' Day and ends on the eve of May Day, begins with a joke and ends with an outdoor sleep-out. Here in Ontario, Canada, the average temperature at the beginning of April is close to freezing. It's common to have snow on the ground. Throughout April a magical transformation occurs: the temperature climbs as high as 66 degrees Fahrenheit (19 degrees Celsius) and flowers bloom.

Post-equinox, the days grow longer. Between April 1 and 30, the daylight increases from 12 hours and 46 minutes to 14 hours and 8 minutes. As the sun travels northward, it climbs in the sky. Not only do days lengthen, but shadows shorten as well. It is inviting to get outdoors. Like the plants that need sunlight to conduct photosynthesis, we humans need sunlight to help manufacture vitamin D.

This month, make time to enjoy the outdoors. Get out in the daylight, take evening walks in the twilight after dinner, contemplate your garden, and turn your face toward the sun at every chance. With winter coming to an end, now is your time to transform.

Dallas Jennifer Cobb

April 1
Wednesday

1st ♋

2nd Quarter 6:21 am

Color of the Day: Topaz
Incense of the Day: Lavender

April Fools' Day – All Fools' Day

Beginner's Luck

In the tarot, the Fool embodies the energy of traipsing off into the unknown with all the courage and, well, foolishness that this can entail! Whenever we embark on something new, we're channeling a little—or a lot—of the Fool, and this is vital energy, for without it we'd never take the risks that allow us to expand and evolve.

Use this spell to call on the beneficial aspects of the Fool before starting something new. Say:

As I embark on this new path,

My senses keen, I need no map.

My higher self will guide me true,

And the Fool brings luck to all I do.

As you continue on this path, be mindful of times when your ego wants to micromanage things, and channel a little dose of Fool energy to break through fear and analysis paralysis, bringing you back into a natural sense of flow and intuitive awareness.

Melissa Tipton

April 2
Thursday

2nd ♋

☽ v/c 12:49 pm

☽ → ♌ 2:26 pm

Color of the Day: Green
Incense of the Day: Nutmeg

Pentacles of Prosperity

The US Congress passed the Coinage Act on this day in 1792 to regulate coin amounts and usages (which at the time included coins called *eagles* and *half eagles*). Coins are associated with pentacles, so this is a great day to use them to grow your prosperity.

Gather these supplies:

• A small green or gold bag

• 1 of each of the following: a penny, nickel, dime, quarter, fifty-cent piece, and dollar coin

• 1 whole nutmeg

Bless the supplies in the name of the prosperity goddess of your choice, such as Habondia, Rosmerta, Fortuna, etc.

As you drop each coin in the bag, from the lowest to the highest denomination, say the following:

From penny to dollar,

My prosperity flowers.

Drop in the nutmeg last. Carry this with you until your prosperity manifests.

Cerridwen Iris Shea

April 3
Friday

2nd ♌

☽ v/c 3:29 pm

Color of the Day: Pink
Incense of the Day: Orchid

Three Cauldron Love Spell

The body has different centers of power. The three most powerful are sometimes envisioned as cauldrons. The cauldron system is Celtic (from the text called the *Cauldron of Poesy*) and is akin to the chakra model though fewer in number. The three cauldrons—the cauldron of incubation (in the belly), the cauldron of motion (in the heart), and the cauldron of wisdom (in the skull)—support vitality, emotions, and wisdom, respectively.

To begin, meditate, visualizing the cauldrons in your body glowing with red (belly), blue-green (heart), and gold (head) light. Turn your focus to your vision of an ideal mate. Send light from your cauldrons to connect to theirs, creating a bond as you say:

Light streams forth from cauldrons filled, with love and magic to merge our fates; through thought, emotion, and power of will, my goal to join with ideal mate; for highest good, harming none, I declare this spell is done.

Michael Furie

April 4
Saturday

2nd ♌

☽ → ♍ 5:18 pm

Color of the Day: Blue
Incense of the Day: Sage

Four Flames Spell

Falling during the time of Aries, this spell calls upon the balancing power of the number four to achieve a solid result.

Gather these items:

• 4 tealight candles

• A small square mirror big enough to rest the candles on

Lay the mirror facing upward on a stable surface and turn it so it makes a diamond shape in front of you. Place a candle at each corner (E, S, W, N), and light each in turn while saying the corresponding line:

Flame of the east, come light the feast.

Flame of the south, be gentle of mouth.

Flame of the west, you know my quest.

Flame of the north, come bring it forth.

Once all are lit, look at the reflection of the flames, with your goal in mind, and say:

Four flames combined,
the power is mine.

Allow the candles to burn out safely, then respectfully dispose of them and place the mirror on or near your altar.

Laura Tempest Zakroff

April 5
Sunday

2nd ♏

Color of the Day: Yellow
Incense of the Day: Marigold

Palm Sunday

Promoting Yourself

As individuals, we're always looking for ways to better our lives. One way we can do that is by working hard and excelling at our chosen path. However, we can sometimes use a little boost to help us out.

Sunday is a good time to harness the energy for a spell to increase your chances of landing a promotion at work. Take your watch, jewelry, or stone (citrine or sunstone) and place it in a bowl during the day to charge in the sun. Before removing it from the bowl, say:

This item will help me in the long run, with the energy from the sun.

Wear or carry the item with you to work as you continue to put yourself in a position for a promotion.

Charlynn Walls

 ## April 6
Monday

2nd ♏

☽ v/c 9:29 am

☽ → ♎ 5:16 pm

Color of the Day: Gray
Incense of the Day: Hyssop

Coworker Sweetener Spell

Having trouble with a coworker? Sweeten them up with this quick and easy spell. You will need a small bottle, an object representing the person you are having trouble with, and some sugar water.

Place the item representing the person you need to sweeten into the bottle. You can write their name on a piece of paper or pick a stone that reminds you of them. (For example, use jade for a person named Jade!) Add water mixed with sugar or honey to your bottle, then seal it with wax, if possible, and anoint it with a positive essential oil (such as tangerine, basil, or lavender), if available.

Take the bottle to work with you and keep it at your work station or in your pocket. The person giving you grief will either end up leaving you alone or actually start treating you with kindness and/or respect.

Ari & Jason Mankey

April 7
Tuesday

2nd ♎

Full Moon 10:35 pm

Color of the Day: White
Incense of the Day: Cinnamon

Recharge!

The full moon is a time of energy. After all, if the moon can pull the earth's oceans from one place to another, imagine how it can affect us! A bedtime ritual of relaxation will help ease your sleep and dreams on this full moon night.

An hour before bed, turn off all screens. Tumble your nightclothes in the dryer for 10–15 minutes; remove them, wrap them tightly in a thick towel, and set aside. Draw a hot bath and scent it with lavender, chamomile, or lemon balm (herbs associated with relaxation) or add your favorite bubble bath or bath bomb. Prepare a cup of caffeine-free tea, and safely light a couple of candles in the bathroom.

Step into the bath and luxuriate in the scent, warmth, and textures. When done, dry off with a clean towel and don your warm pajamas. Slip into bed, saying:

Saint Calgon, take me away.

Ease into untroubled sleep.
                              Susan Pesznecker

▽ **April 8**
Wednesday

3rd ♎

☽ v/c 8:50 am

☽ → ♏ 4:17 pm

Color of the Day: Brown
Incense of the Day: Lilac

Cool as a Cucumber

There's an odd saying, "cool as a cucumber," which means to be calm and completely chilled out. Supposedly this saying originates from the fact that the inside of a cucumber is always cold, even on the hottest summer day.

To make a refreshing, healthy drink that will also spread peaceful vibes, chop a cucumber into round slices. On each slice, carefully carve a peace symbol into one side, using the natural round rind of the vegetable as the circle part of the design. See each slice glow with calm white energy. Add the rounds to a pitcher of water, chill, and serve.

You can make this any time you need to bring calm energies into yourself after a heated discussion or situation. If you don't enjoy drinking water, you can just eat the slices of cucumber instead. Cucumbers are high in vitamin B_5 and are good for your skin!

                              Kate Freuler

April 9
Thursday

3rd ♏

Color of the Day: Crimson
Incense of the Day: Mulberry

Passover begins (at sundown on April 8)

Passover Meal

Last night at sundown, Passover began, making today the first day of Passover: the holiday that commemorates the Jewish liberation from slavery in Egypt. In recent years, it has become increasingly popular for non-Jewish populations, particularly oppressed minorities, to hold a *seder* (a Passover meal) to honor liberation in various forms. President Obama began the tradition of having a White House seder meal, which included a recitation of the Emancipation Proclamation.

Today, learn about the history and customs of Passover and plan your own seder meal to respect past struggles and celebrate liberation you've experienced personally or that has been experienced by your ancestors or historical groups with whom you share a common bond (such as an ethnic group, a spiritual community, or the LGBTQ community). Some traditional aspects of the seder meal include matzo ball soup, four glasses of wine, and the absence of leavened bread.

Tess Whitehurst

April 10
Friday

3rd ♏

☽ v/c 3:35 pm
☽ → ♐ 4:35 pm

Color of the Day: Rose
Incense of the Day: Violet

Good Friday

A Spell for Love

In many cultures, this is a sacred and holy day. Even if this isn't your tradition, there's still plenty of magic to be found! This spell harnesses the energy of the moon to help you find your authentic empowerment. You'll need a mirror, some sage, and a small piece of cotton cloth.

Look into the mirror and rub the sage between your palms. As you do this, say these words:

Love in front of me,

Love behind me,

Love above me,

Love below me,

Love around me,

Love within me,

All my life is love.

Wrap the sage in the cloth. Keep it somewhere personal and private, as a reminder that any day of the week, you're surrounded by divine love.

Charlie Rainbow Wolf

April 11
Saturday

3rd ♐

Color of the Day: Indigo
Incense of the Day: Sandalwood

A Lavender Asperging Spell

Lavender is a plant associated with love, purity, cleansing, and higher vibrations. Cultivate or purchase a sprig of lavender for this cleansing spell. Additionally, mix up a bowl of fresh spring water and sea salt.

Pinch some of the lavender with your fingers. Inhale its gorgeous scent deeply, and before exhaling, declare:

> *I cleanse and purify with
> the glory of nature.*

Dip the sprig into the salt water and sprinkle (asperge) any room, item, person, or pet that you wish to bless. With each sprinkle, you may wish to recite a positive mantra or affirmation, or simply say *blessed be*.

You may be drawn to bless your bedroom, vehicle, front door, technological items, garden, or anything else toward which your intuition guides you. If you wish to bless something from afar, simply use a photo or other representation of that person or place.

Raven Digitalis

April 12
Sunday

3rd ♐

☽ v/c 7:46 am

☽ → ♑ 8:05 pm

Color of the Day: Gold
Incense of the Day: Hyacinth

Easter

Eggscellent Spell

People of many traditions like to dye eggs at this time of year, so if you find yourself with a surplus of hard-boiled colored eggs and you have a garden, this is a fun spell to do to put them to use.

After using the insides of the eggs for food or offerings, save the eggshells and let them dry. Once dry, use a mortar and pestle to grind them up into smaller, gravel-like particles. Once you have processed them all, disperse them outside in your flower beds or pots, circling your home in a clockwise fashion as you go, focusing on blessing and protecting your home and family. The eggshells will add nutrients to the earth while also deterring certain kinds of garden pests—and will add some fun color!

Laura Tempest Zakroff

April 13
Monday

3rd ♑

Color of the Day: Ivory
Incense of the Day: Neroli

A Spell to Quiet the Mind

Mercury recently entered the sign of Aries, heightening our intuition and encouraging us to bring forth our inner truth and share it with the world. Cast this spell to quiet the mind and bring focus to your thoughts so you can find that inner truth.

Sit comfortably and focus on your breath for a few minutes, relaxing the body and opening the mind. Visualize the symbol of Aries (♈) made of light-blue liquid fire, hovering above your head, and say:

Aries blue and liquid fire, balance of thought is my desire.

Take three deep breaths and visualize the symbol descending into your third eye, where it is absorbed. Repeat as necessary.

Devin Hunter

April 14
Tuesday

3rd ♑
4th Quarter 6:56 pm
☽ v/c 7:47 pm

Color of the Day: Red
Incense of the Day: Bayberry

End a Curse Spell

Let the renewing April rain help you clear away any negative magic with this spell. If you think you're the victim of a curse, perform this spell on a rainy day. You'll need one lemon, a knife, and black peppercorns in a grinder. (These can be found in any supermarket.)

Think of the problem you're having. If you know the source of the curse, think about that. But don't direct this spell at anyone specific. After thinking about the curse, gash the lemon in several places. Grind some pepper over the lemon and rub it into the gashes. Take the lemon to a secluded spot or a compost pile. Smash, step on, or bury the lemon as you say:

Pepper sting, rain and lemon cleanse,

By my command, this curse now ends.

Simply walk away. The curse's power will begin to weaken.

James Kambos

 ## April 15
Wednesday

4↑↓ ♑

☽ → ♒ 3:37 am

Color of the Day: Yellow
Incense of the Day: Bay laurel

Ebb and Flow Tax Blessing

Tax season can be stressful. The positive side of taxes is that they support infrastructure, education, the arts, etc.

On Tax Day, as you sign and seal your return, say this three times:

I pay my fair share,

I support my tribe;

I receive my fair share,

And balance the vibe.

Send your return off and forget about it. Then pour yourself a favorite beverage and relax!

Cerridwen Iris Shea

 ## April 16
Thursday

4↑↓ ♒

Color of the Day: Turquoise
Incense of the Day: Clove

Passover ends

Protection Charm for Vulnerable Ones

This time of year can be especially challenging for those with preteens or other loved ones who are vulnerable to rampaging sexual energies, both from within and without!

For this spell, start by making or purchasing a cotton pouch of a color and design that will be pleasing to the young person (so they'll actually wear it!). To seal the spell, blend together the following herbs (or suitable substitutes):

- Rose
- Pine
- Cedar
- Nutmeg
- Ginger
- Lavender
- Lemon
- Yarrow
- Mugwort

- Sage (culinary)
- Barley
- Echinacea

Blend the herbs together in a bowl while focusing deeply on a bright, strong protective circle growing outward from the mixture.

Place a small crystal and a cowrie shell (for the balance of male and female energies) into the pouch first, followed by a generous pinch of the herbs. Save the rest of the herbs for replacing as needed.

When presenting the charm to your loved one, remind them that they are the only person who gets to decide who gets close to, touches, or advises them.

Thuri Calafia

 April 17
Friday

4th ♒
☽ v/c 10:34 am
☽ → ♓ 2:29 pm

Color of the Day: Coral
Incense of the Day: Orchid

Relax and Enjoy It

It's mid-spring (or, if you're in the Southern Hemisphere, mid-fall), the weather is no doubt sunny and mild, all's good at home or work…but you're too busy to enjoy a lovely day. You need a brief vacation so you can enjoy at least this day of your life.

Take a deep, easy breath and relax. Then do it again. Close your eyes and "look" at this day and see what blessings it's bringing you. Take another deep, easy breath and open your eyes. Consider the Three Graces (sometimes called the Charities), who are the daughters of Zeus and companions to the Muses. The Graces are Thalia (youth and beauty), Euphrosyne (mirth), and Aglaia (elegance). Go online and find any of the dozens of paintings and statues of them. Invoke them:

Loving Graces, you're bringing joy to my life

And teaching me to relax and dance and sing.

Thank you, thank you, thank you!

Barbara Ardinger

April 18
Saturday

4th ♓

Color of the Day: Brown
Incense of the Day: Patchouli

Blessing Your Plants

Whether we have a single houseplant or a full garden, a blessing over our plants can give a nice boost of energy, encouraging them to grow and thrive. For indoor plants, they can be gathered together on a table or the blessing can be repeated going from plant to plant in the home. For an outdoor garden, a circuit can be made around the perimeter as the blessing is given.

To perform the blessing, hold out your dominant hand and visualize bright green energy streaming from your hand and up from the earth to surround the plants, bathing them in the light of healing, growth, fertility, and abundance, while saying (or thinking):

Strength and growth, these powers shine, to give this flora vitality; blessed in abundance and magic divine, as I will, so mote it be.

Michael Furie

▽ **April 19**
Sunday

4th ♓
☉ → ♉ 10:45 am
☽ v/c 7:31 pm

Color of the Day: Amber
Incense of the Day: Almond

Wordless Magic

We often think that casting spells requires words, but here you'll explore the power of your body as you weave wordless magic. Decide on the desired outcome of your spell, such as eating healthier, a fulfilling job, and so forth. Be specific. Then brainstorm ways to physically act out this desired outcome.

For many of us, kinesthetic awareness can be more difficult to tap into, so allow yourself to play and experiment without judgment. One way to start is to pantomime the actions of your goal; for example, choosing and preparing healthy meals or performing satisfying job functions. As you move, notice how you feel, both bodily sensations and emotions, and allow these energies to fuel your magic as you focus on the desired outcome.

When the movements feel complete, take a few breaths in stillness and silence, and cultivate gratitude for the unfolding of your spell in a manner that is perfect for you in every way.

Melissa Tipton

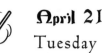

 ## April 20
Monday

4th ♓

☽ → ♈ 3:00 am

Color of the Day: Gray
Incense of the Day: Clary sage

Self-Esteem Bath Spell

Start this spell by writing down the things that bother you about yourself. Follow this up by drawing a bath. As the water runs, add some cleansing essential oils to the bathwater (suggested oils: sandalwood, jasmine, ylang-ylang, and clary sage), along with some rose petals for self-love. Pour yourself a glass of wine, if desired, and play some of your favorite music in the background.

As you settle into the tub, relax and feel the negative feelings you have about yourself being washed away by the bathwater. Before getting out of the tub, make sure you've washed away everything on your list.

When you feel cleansed, emerge from the water and look into your bathroom mirror. View yourself free of the things that previously bothered you, saying:

This is how I and others will see me.

As I will it, so shall it be!

Ari & Jason Mankey

April 21
Tuesday

4th ♈

Color of the Day: Black
Incense of the Day: Basil

Storm Spell

Next time a rain shower occurs, take a bowl outdoors and spend some time in the downpour. Find a spot where the bowl will gather raindrops. (Under a downspout works.) Close your eyes and feel a connection with the storm. Contemplate the clouds as they shed their weight and then drift off, light and free. Feel how the rain washes over the earth and trees, dragging away the unneeded debris. Ask the storm to lend its force to your ritual and thank it for the cleansing water.

At bedtime, place the bowl of water under your bed. The rain inside of it has the power to drain negative vibrations off you and cleanse your energy, just as it cleansed and nourished the outdoors. Sleep with it under your bed and awaken refreshed. Dump the water out in the morning.

Kate Freuler

April 22
Wednesday

4th ♈

☽ v/c 8:32 am

☽ → ♉ 3:36 pm

New Moon 10:26 pm

Color of the Day: White

Incense of the Day: Marjoram

Earth Day

Renewing the Earth

Pagans are connected to the earth and its natural cycles. We feel that bond, and today it is especially notable as it is Earth Day. Today we work to preserve the land for future generations. Our planet has sustained many blows at the hands of human-kind. With the energies of today's new moon, we can work to reverse the circumstances that created the damage.

Find a small ball, marble, or round rock to represent the earth. Take a piece of orange paper or cloth and cover the ball, which will work with and utilize the energies of the day of the week and encourage change. Hold the covered ball in your hands and visualize the waters of the earth run-ning clear, the land strong, and the air clean. Then remove the covering as you visualize the impurities moving from the ball into the cloth. Wash the cloth or burn the paper and the spell is complete.

Charlynn Walls

 April 23
Thursday

1st ♉

Color of the Day: Green

Incense of the Day: Balsam

Ramadan begins

Fast from Food but Not from Charity

Ramadan, which begins tonight, is a holy month. With specific exceptions, people fast and avoid sin-ful behavior from dawn to sunset, then feast at night. They engage in prayer both day and night.

Pagans are not cultural pirates. We do not steal other people's observances and beliefs. But we can follow the Islamic tradition of doing charitable works, not just this month but all year. Send blessings of peace and good hope to our Muslim cousins and observe this holy month in your own way. Recite this blessing today and perhaps every morning until May 23:

As I fast from food, I know there's more for those in need.

As I meditate, I know that goodness and peace go out into the world.

As I donate or volunteer where help is needed, I know that others will receive.

I send blessings to my cousins of every faith throughout the world.

Barbara Ardinger

April 24
Friday

1st ♉

☽ v/c 8:43 pm

Color of the Day: Purple
Incense of the Day: Cypress

Love-Drawing Perfume

On this Venus-ruled Friday, with the moon in Venus-ruled Taurus, it's the perfect day to make this earthy, love-drawing perfume. You will need the following:

- 10 drops vetiver essential oil
- 5 drops patchouli essential oil
- 5 drops vanilla essential oil
- A 5 ml glass bottle
- A quartz crystal point
- Sweet almond oil

Combine the essential oils in the glass bottle. Close the lid and shake gently. Then bury it at the base of a tree (ideally in your yard or the yard of someone you know so it won't be disturbed) to let it absorb the deep, sensual energies of Mother Earth. Place the quartz crystal point on top to mark the bottle's location and further empower it with magic.

In seven days, dig up the bottle, wash off the dirt, and fill it the rest of the way with sweet almond oil. Shake gently to combine. Apply to your wrists, belly, and heart to attract romantic attention, enhance sexual attraction, and help magnetize the love you desire.

Tess Whitehurst

April 25
Saturday

1st ♉

☽ → ♊ 3:20 am

Color of the Day: Black
Incense of the Day: Pine

A handprint "Come to Me" Spell

Acquire some ink or a natural dye with which you can make a handprint on a large piece of paper. I suggest mixing powdered turmeric root or beetroot with water, or research how to create natural coloring by utilizing different plant materials.

Dip your right hand in the mixture and press it firmly to the middle of the paper. As you are doing so, imagine your projective energy entering the print with a superboost of power.

After washing your hands, take a marker and write symbols and words that are aligned with your manifestations on the print. For example, you may draw dollar signs and smiley faces, or perhaps create your own symbols and sigils aimed at increasing abundance on numerous levels: mentally, emotionally, physically, and spiritually.

Enchant this piece however you would like, ideally giving it at least one day of pure sunlight by placing it securely outside. You may wish to keep this piece as a magickal focal item, or you may wish to burn it in a sacred Beltane fire.

Raven Digitalis

April 26
Sunday

1st ♊

Color of the Day: Yellow
Incense of the Day: Frankincense

A Spell for Household Protection

This spell is so easy, you'll wonder why you haven't been doing it for ages! You'll need a household broom and some coarse sea salt.

Using the broom, go through every room of your house and sweep up the floor. Keep sweeping until you're at an outside door. Open the door and sweep everything outside. Keep sweeping until everything is off your property! If you have carpets, just go through the motion of sweeping everything up. Remember, it's your intent that's important, not how much you actually collect. Don't forget to go into corners and under furniture.

Once you've swept anything negative or unwanted outside and off your property, sprinkle some salt on either side of the threshold of the door. As you do so, say these words:

Salt of the earth and salt from the sea,

*Protect my home and dwelling,
times three!*

Spin around clockwise three times, and you're finished!

Charlie Rainbow Wolf

April 27
Monday

1st ♊

☽ v/c 1:00 pm

☽ → ♋ 1:28 pm

Color of the Day: Silver
Incense of the Day: Narcissus

A Spell for Releasing the Past

As the day begins, the moon is in Gemini, bringing up memories from our past, both good and bad. Cast this spell to release any people or experiences from the past that you might be holding onto, and reclaim your power. You will need a piece of paper, a pen, a fire or fireplace, and something to smudge with afterward.

With the paper and pen, write out in detail what the memory is and how it has affected you, and list the names of the people involved. Next to the fire, read aloud what you have written, then say three things that you can do in the present to release the energetic and emotional ties to the memory.

After you have done this, toss the paper in the fire and say:

I choose to be free, I choose to forgive.

Unburden my heart for as long as I live!

Smudge yourself afterward to finish the working.

Devin Hunter

April 28
Tuesday

1st ♋

Color of the Day: Scarlet
Incense of the Day: Geranium

Miracle of Spring Spell

The miracle of spring is all around us now. What was once a mist of green on the trees has turned into a leafy canopy. What was once a bare stem now bears flowers. Let this season of growth inspire your spellwork. This spell will help any wish come true. You'll need a pale green candle and a holder, paper, and a pen.

First, think of your wish and write it down. Then light the candle. As you sit before the candle, speak your wish aloud, then say this charm:

> *Trees are in leaf, flowers*
> *bloom, buds swell.*
>
> *Let the life force of nature feed my spell.*

Let the candle burn for a while, then snuff it out. Repeat this spell three nights in a row. Hide your wish until it comes true, then discard it. Use the candle again for other growth spells.

James Kambos

♥ **April 29**
Wednesday

1st ♋

☽ v/c 3:29 pm
☽ → ♌ 9:06 pm

Color of the Day: Brown
Incense of the Day: Honeysuckle

Seed Blessing

Spring is the perfect time for a seed blessing ritual. A few days or weeks before the ritual, shop for or select the seeds you wish to use. Choose a full-sun day for the ritual. Just after sunrise, fill a treasured or blessed bowl with a bit of garden or potting soil, then set the seeds or packets in the bowl. (Wrap loose seeds in a bit of tissue.) Holding the bowl in your hands, face east, lift the bowl toward the sun, and intone:

> *Blessed sun and mother Gaia,*
>
> *Hold these seeds close to your breast.*
>
> *Fire and earth bring fertile life,*
>
> *Air and water inspire the rest.*

Leave the seeds in the direct sunshine until sunset (if your home area is too hot to leave them in direct sun, use a sunny window), then tuck them into a corner of your altar space until it's time to plant them.

Susan Pesznecker

April 30
Thursday

1st ♈ ♌

2nd Quarter 4:38 pm

Color of the Day: Purple
Incense of the Day: Jasmine

Bringing in the May Spell

In many Witchcraft traditions, Beltane is April 30, or May Eve. To enhance and bring these bright, loving energies into your life, first take a small blade or wooden pick and inscribe and then anoint a purple candle with symbols of passion, ardor, and love. You can use a simple oil, such as olive, which has been blessed previously, or if you have another oil you prefer, such as an essential oil, dress your candle with that by tracing the symbols you carved.

Safely light the candle and focus on all the things you like about yourself, how special and unique you are, and what you have to offer to love. Allow your imagination to wander, and don't scrimp on the praise.

Stand in the shape of a star, with arms and legs extended in a stance of receptivity and healthy self-esteem. Now focus on those energies and qualities in others that you wish to draw to you. Chant the following nine times:

To me, to me! Energies of passion

And truth and love in accord.

May love find me shining and standing strong

That my tribe will find their way home.

In the coming days, stay open and receptive to the new people who come into your life. Even if someone isn't your usual type, you might be surprised at what you'll learn about them, the world, and yourself. Blessed be.

Thuri Calafia

May

Welcome to the famously merry month of May! Though it was originally named after the Greek fertility goddess Maia, the Catholic Church has since designated this month as sacred to the Virgin Mary, even referring to her as "the Queen of May" during this time. Day one of this flower-filled month is the beloved holiday of Beltane, during which the veil that usually conceals the world of the fairies fades, and our power to make contact with them reaches its yearly peak. Indeed, May's birth flower is a fairy favorite: the lily of the valley. As for our skies, this month they host the Eta Aquariids meteor shower, which reaches its peak around May 6 and is most visible before the sunrise.

May is also the month when the light half of the year begins to assert itself in earnest, and we sense the days lengthening, the sun growing warmer, and the leaves filling out the trees. This allows us to gaze bravely into our own brilliance and to courageously release anything that has been holding us back from being our most radiant, expansive, beautiful selves. Indeed, May's bright presence reminds us to claim the vital prosperity that is our birthright and our natural state.

Tess Whitehurst

May 1
Friday

2nd ♌

☽ v/c 12:04 pm

Color of the Day: Rose
Incense of the Day: Thyme

Beltane

A Beltane Purifying Spell

Beltane is a good time to purify and cleanse your life of excess emotional baggage or problems. For this ritual, you'll need your cauldron, white paper, and a red ink pen.

Begin by building a small ritual fire in the cauldron. Hold your hands over the fire and feel its energy. Then write any problems or issues you'd like to get rid of on the paper. Read what you've written out loud. Tear the paper into small pieces and toss them into the cauldron. Watch the flames consume the paper, destroying your problems and cleansing your life. As the smoke rises, say:

Beltane fire, burn,
Beltane fire, purify,

Carry my problems away
until they reach the sky.

After the ashes have cooled, sprinkle them on the ground as an offering.

James Kambos

May 2
Saturday

2nd ♌

☽ → ♍ 1:35 am

Color of the Day: Brown
Incense of the Day: Ivy

Renewing Your Bond with the Land

The land is green and life is abundant again. Now is the time to reaffirm and renew your bond with the land. This can be especially important if you are in a new home or if you have created a garden and you need to establish a connection that creates a give-and-take and bonds you to the land.

You will need to be outside in the space that you want to create a connection with. Taking off your shoes and kneeling on the land will allow you to place your hands on the soil and create a good connection. Close your eyes and slow your breathing. Listen to the land that surrounds you and breathe in that energy. As you exhale, push your energy into the land. Do that give-and-take several times. When you find that it is hard to know where one ends and the other begins, that is when you know the connection is complete!

Charlynn Walls

May 3
Sunday

2nd ♏

☽ v/c 10:25 pm

Color of the Day: Gold
Incense of the Day: Almond

Panacea Charm

To support physical healing from any injury or ailment, for yourself or a loved one, empower a clear quartz in bright sunlight. (On a cloudy day, bathe it in the light from a candle flame.) Then, with ribbon, tie it into a scrap of green flannel, along with a pinch of dried calendula, a pinch of dried yarrow, and a whole clove of garlic. Hold the charm in your right hand and invoke Panacea, the goddess of universal remedy, by saying:

> Panacea, I invoke your all-encompassing power to cure and to heal. Please bless this charm with your power, and restore me (or the name of a loved one) to perfect health. Thank you.

Feel the charm pulsating with Panacea's radiant, enveloping power. Keep the charm near you (or instruct your loved one to do so) until the desired healing has occurred. Then release the contents to a moving body of water and discard the flannel and ribbon.

Tess Whitehurst

May 4
Monday

2nd ♏

☽ → ♎ 3:09 am

Color of the Day: Ivory
Incense of the Day: Rosemary

Primp My Ride

Taking time to cleanse and clear your preferred mode of travel, be it car, bike, shoes, etc., is a powerful way to remove obstructions to forward movement in your life.

Start with a physical cleaning. Declutter, vacuum, and wash your car; wash your bike and oil the chain; clean or polish your shoes. Then use your energetic cleanser of choice, such as sage smoke or spray, copal or sandalwood incense, Reiki, a salt water sprinkling, etc. For added oomph, put a cleansed quartz crystal (cleanse the crystal by placing in a bowl of salt overnight; discard salt) in your car or tie a quartz pendant to your bike or shoelace.

Charge your mode of transportation with the following:

> I charge this/these (car/bike/shoes, etc.) to be a vehicle for safe travel, always taking me to the right place at the right time.

Happy travels!

Melissa Tipton

May 5
Tuesday

2nd ♎

☽ v/c 10:31 pm

Color of the Day: Red
Incense of the Day: Cinnamon

Cinco de Mayo

A Makeup Spell for Emotional Balance

Regardless of your sexual or gender identity, procure a bit of makeup for this spell. Whether it's eyeshadow, eyeliner, lipstick, or something else, you will be applying this makeup as a private magickal act. This is not about appearance.

Begin by calling your guides and guardians however you see fit. Visualize yourself surrounded by a white flame of purification. As you apply the makeup to your eyes, say:

My vision is purified; I see myself and others with greater clarity and ease.

Apply makeup to your lips and say:

I speak clearly and wisely; my intentions and views are lovingly communicated.

Feel free to take this a step further by applying makeup to your ears and forehead to invoke clarity of mind and perception. Follow your intuition!

After washing off the makeup, declare:

My emotions are balanced, purified, and clear!

Incorporate any additional affirmations or spoken spells as you see fit.

Raven Digitalis

May 6
Wednesday

2nd ♎︎

☽ → ♏︎ 3:05 am

Color of the Day: Topaz
Incense of the Day: Bay laurel

Pomegranate Wishing Spell

The pomegranate appears over and over again in mythology and is considered a mystical fruit. Some say it has the power to grant wishes when eaten.

Cut open a pomegranate and remove the seeds one by one. Place them on a plate in a shape or pattern representing your wish. Some ideas include a dollar sign for money, a heart for love, a spiral for spirituality, or an X for protection. Focus on the seed design and imagine that your wish has already been granted and how you would feel to have what you desire. Let that feeling flow from your heart center into the pomegranate seeds, filling them up with power. Then eat the seeds one by one, all the while holding onto the feeling of realizing your goal.

Know that your spell is working as your body absorbs the mythological powers of the pomegranate.

Kate Freuler

May 7
Thursday

2nd ♏︎

🌕 Full Moon 6:45 am

☽ v/c 10:39 pm

Color of the Day: Green
Incense of the Day: Apricot

Full Moon Scrying Spell

Beltane is opposite Samhain on the Wheel of the Year, and this full moon, so close to Beltane, is excellent for scrying.

Use a scrying mirror or a dark bowl filled with water. Safely light a purple candle and lilac incense. Turn out the lights in the room and close the curtains. Make sure you will not be interrupted for at least thirty minutes.

Follow your breath to relax.

Focus softly on the scrying tool. Breathe. Let the images form in the glass or water. If you have a specific question, ask it. Otherwise, simply observe.

When the images fade, write them down in your magical journal before you forget, then extinguish the candle (or let it burn down). Ground by placing your palms on the earth. Feel any excess energy flow out, and the stability of the earth beneath you. Pour out the water somewhere outside.

Attune to any dreams or experiences that connect to the images, and meditate on them for interpretation.

Cerridwen Iris Shea

May 8
Friday

3rd ♏

☽ → ♐ 3:15 am

Color of the Day: White
Incense of the Day: Mint

Shoot for the Stars Spell

Today is a great time to dream big about our goals and our future, as the sun's strength is waxing and the moon is just past full. What is it that you've always wanted? No dream is too big on a bright spring day like today!

Allow the energy of your most treasured goal to fill you as you visualize yourself living within that dream. Light a candle of the color that best represents your goal, and build energy by chanting:

*To the brightest stars
now, my aim is true,*

*For I've given my all and
I've paid my dues,*

*So the best of everything
now comes to me,*

*By the grace of the gods!
So mote it be!*

When the power peaks, visualize gold and silver sparks falling from the stars, entering your body, and merging with your own energy, making you stronger, more powerful, and more capable of reaching those stars! Let the candle safely burn down completely, knowing that you can and will achieve your goal.

Thuri Calafia

May 9
Saturday

3rd ♐

Color of the Day: Blue
Incense of the Day: Magnolia

Self-Care Bath Spell

In the Major Arcana of the Tarot, the number nine rests with the Hermit. The Hermit reminds us to take care of ourselves and to retreat from the world now and then.

For this spell, gather these ingredients:

- 2 tablespoons dried lavender
- Approximately 4 leaves of sage (fresh or dried)
- 1 teaspoon sea salt
- 1 teaspoon honey
- A cotton satchel or tea bag to hold everything

Place the ingredients in the satchel in this order, saying:

Lavender to calm my body,

Sage to clear my mind,

Salt to cleanse my spirit,

Honey to soothe my heart.

Next, add the satchel to your bath or place it in the shower stream and enjoy!

Laura Tempest Zakroff

May 10
Sunday

3rd ♐

☽ v/c 2:11 am

☽ → ♑ 5:39 am

Color of the Day: Orange
Incense of the Day: Eucalyptus

Mother's Day

To Share Love with Someone You Care About

As we grow older, we often find ourselves separated from those we care about on holidays like Mother's Day. Here's a way to send them a magickal hug to let them know they are in our thoughts.

Start by placing a picture of your mother (or other loved one) on your altar's pentacle, along with an item that connects them to you (such as a gift they've given you). If you happen to have a piece of rose quartz handy, place that on top of your pentacle too. Pentacles are magickal gateways, and placing at least two of these items upon it should connect you to your loved one.

In order to share the love you're feeling, sprinkle rose water (or rose petals) upon your loved one's picture. They should be able to feel your feelings and thoughts as you do this and will know that you care.

Ari & Jason Mankey

May 11
Monday

3rd ♑

Color of the Day: Lavender
Incense of the Day: Neroli

Olde May Day

Though dates vary from tradition to tradition, an older date for the Beltane celebration would fall on this day rather than our modern standard of April 30/May 1. An easy way to help tune into and harness the energy present at this time is to spend as much of the day outdoors as you can, whether it be to have a barbeque, work in a garden, or hold a formal ritual. If possible, meditate for a time outdoors, and as you breathe in and out, visualize yourself breathing in the energy of Beltane and exhaling anything unhealthy or incorrect for you.

Michael Furie

May 12
Tuesday

3rd ♑

☽ v/c 6:30 am
☽ → ♒ 11:39 am

Color of the Day: White
Incense of the Day: Cedar

Spell for Psychic Dreaming

The moon enters Aquarius today, bringing with it the power of prophecy, enhanced empathy, and psychic fortitude. Cast this spell tonight to encourage and intensify your psychic dreaming experience.

Before you go to sleep, take a cleansing bath and dry off with a white towel. Place your pillow on your lap, and using the index finger of your dominant hand, draw a giant X across the pillow. As you do, this say:

> An X marks the spot where
> I lay my head, the place I
> dream when I go to bed.
>
> Here I focus prophecy and
> light, where I summon the
> visions from night.
>
> Hear my words and make
> them so, where I place this
> X, the power shall flow!

When you wake up, be sure to write down any dreams you had and ask your spirit guides for help in deciphering their meaning.

Devin Hunter

May 13
Wednesday

3rd ♒

Color of the Day: Yellow
Incense of the Day: Lavender

honoring the Blessed Virgin Mary

After the death of her son, Mary Theotokos (Mother of God) retired to Ephesus. In 1950, her bodily assumption into heaven was declared by Pope Pius XII. In 1997, Catholics around the world petitioned Pope John Paul II to proclaim her a "Co-Redeemer, Mediatrix of All Graces, and Advocate for the people of God." By a vote of 23–0, a Vatican commission advised against this. Mary is not a goddess, but a mother who loves to visit her children—she's appeared and been seen hundreds of times in Europe, Africa, and the Americas.

Honor Mary today by buying a glass jar candle with her picture on it. Set the candle on your altar. Add Tarot card III, the Empress, which can represent Mary as easily as it can represent any goddess. Light the candle and contemplate the card and see where your inner vision goes with this mother of a god.

Barbara Ardinger

NOTES:

May 14
Thursday

3rd ♒

☽ v/c 10:03 am

4th Quarter 10:03 am

☽ → ♓ 9:24 pm

Color of the Day: Turquoise
Incense of the Day: Carnation

Catching Dreams

Make an inspirational dream catcher to bring your dreams to fruition! You'll need:

- 8 six-inch sticks, dowels, or twigs
- Natural-fiber string
- Crystal beads or small totems (garnet, lapis, citrine, labradorite, or malachite—or substitutes of like color)
- Small items you associate with success or prosperity
- A small pad of paper
- A pencil

Lash the sticks together firmly at their centers, like spokes in a wheel. If you're not comfortable with lashing, hot glue will work. Tie your string to the center of one spoke and begin weaving over and under the others, working clockwise, spider web–style, and leaving space between the threads.

As you work, add in your crystal beads and items. Knot the string when done, adding a loop for hanging.

Hang the dream catcher over your bed. Before sleeping, sit before it and meditate on your hopes of success. Then sleep and dream. When you awaken, immediately record your dream memories on paper.

Susan Pesznecker

May 15
Friday

4f♄ ♓

Color of the Day: Pink
Incense of the Day: Vanilla

A Spell for Fertility

Fertility isn't only the conception of a child. It applies to any area of your life where you want to sow seeds and watch them grow, whether it's a garden or a new project, or even when you're ready for some self-improvement. This spell encompasses all of that and more.

You'll need a candle (preferably white), something to light it with, and some sage or sage incense in a heatproof container or holder.

Light the candle and say these words:

Fire fleet and candlelight,

Hear the prayer I make tonight.

Let me stretch and let me grow,

By light and smoke, I make it so!

Light the sage or incense with the flame from the candle. Pinch out the flame and let the smoke from the incense rise to take your spell out into the universe so that it may return back to you in its fullness.

Charlie Rainbow Wolf

May 16
Saturday

4f♄ ♓

Color of the Day: Gray
Incense of the Day: Rue

Magickal Cleanup

When we have clean spaces, we think and function better. It stands to reason that we would benefit from doing a magickal cleanup of our ritual spaces and our past magickal workings. Today is also a Saturday, which provides the added benefit of aiding our ability to clean up any magickal messes that we may have created.

The first thing you need to do is cleanse your ritual space. Dust, sweep, and tidy up the area. Next, clean up any items from past magickal workings. If there have been items burnt or used up, make sure to bury the ashes or otherwise dispose of them. Finally, if there are any magickal workings in progress that are causing distress, then center yourself, concentrate on that work, and very firmly say:

Let nothing else add to the murk,
cancel and clear this work.

Now both your physical and your magickal spaces are clear.

Charlynn Walls

May 17
Sunday

4th ♓

☽ v/c 3:59 am

☽ → ♈ 9:36 am

Color of the Day: Yellow
Incense of the Day: Hyacinth

Earth Protection Spell

Get a photo of a person or thing you wish to protect from harm. Gather a handful of dirt—any dirt at all—and sprinkle it around the picture in a circle. Say:

Earth and stone to build a wall,

Create a place to hide.

Strong as mountains, hard as rock,

Protecting what's inside.

Whatever or whoever you are guarding from harm will be protected and "hidden" from negative influences until the danger has passed.

Kate Freuler

May 18
Monday

4th ♈

Color of the Day: Gray
Incense of the Day: Lily

Victoria Day (Canada)

Message in a Bottle Spell

To achieve a secret desire, try this spell. You'll need a piece of paper, a pen, and a small clean bottle or jar with a lid. Any clean pill bottle or jar will do.

Write your wish (message) on the paper. Fold the paper and place it in the bottle, then put on the lid. Leave the paper in the bottle for three days. Meditate on your wish each day. On the third day, hold the bottle as you say this charm:

Inside this bottle, my
secret wish is sealed,

No one knows this desire I feel.

Now the time has come to pass,

My wish is released at last!

Remove the "message" from the bottle, and lay it upon your altar. The spell is released and now working in the unseen realm. When your wish comes true, thank the divine power. Discard the paper and keep the bottle for future use.

James Kambos

May 19
Tuesday

4th ♈

☽ v/c 4:33 pm

☽ → ♉ 10:10 pm

Color of the Day: Black
Incense of the Day: Ylang-ylang

Cutting Ties Spell

Sometimes in life, we end up in relationships that are not in our best interest. Cutting those ties can be challenging but necessary in order for us to become our best selves. For this spell, you'll need:

- 1 black candle for yourself
- 1 black candle for the person with whom you are cutting ties
- Candle holders
- A small knife or wooden pick
- A length of black thread or cotton string
- A blessed pair of scissors or small blade

On the candle representing the other person, use a small knife or wooden pick to carve symbols and words representing the behaviors that are no longer acceptable to you. On your personal candle, carve words or symbols describing how you feel when you're around the person.

Place the candles in holders on your altar, then take the black thread and tie one end of it around each candle. Focus on the energies of the person as you light their candle. Speak honestly about the reasons you're letting them go. When the energy peaks, take a blessed pair of scissors or small blade and cut the thread between you, saying:

I forgive you for the behavior that has caused me such pain, but I am no longer willing to accept any more of it! Be gone from my life! So mote it be!

Thuri Calafia

May 20
Wednesday

4th ♉

☉ → ♊ 9:49 am

Color of the Day: White
Incense of the Day: Marjoram

Igniting Abundance

While we often associate abundance strictly with favorable things, abundance is simply a large quantity of something. So instead of requesting general abundance, begin by choosing a specific quality, thing, or experience that you'd like more of. You'll need three to five candles of any type in holders. Feel free to choose a color that matches your intention, such as green for money, pink for love, etc. Bring your focus quality to mind as you light the first candle, saying:

I ignite the quality of (fill in the blank) in my life.

Breathe this quality in, then use the first candle to light the next, saying:

The quality of (fill in the blank) expands within my life in a manner that is perfect for me on all levels.

Repeat this process of breathing in the ever-expanding energy as you continue to light each candle from the previous one. When done, let the candles burn out naturally if possible.

Melissa Tipton

May 21
Thursday

4th ♉

Color of the Day: Crimson
Incense of the Day: Balsam

World Card Travel Spell

If you're planning on going on a trip soon, tap into the blessings of the World card of the Tarot to make the most of your journey. The World card (number 21) represents the completion of the Major Arcana that started with the Fool card at zero, so knowledge has been gathered along the way.

Pull the World card from your deck (or print out an image of it) and situate it upon your altar for the duration of the trip. Say the following blessing (substitute *we/our* if others are traveling with you):

As I go on this trip, I ask the World to guide my way,

May the path be clear and blessed with joy each day.

Use your wisdom to keep me safe and sound,

With the smoothest road always found.

Whether I journey high or journey low,

May I return to the home I know.

Laura Tempest Zakroff

May 22
Friday

4th ♉
☽ v/c 4:01 am
☽ → ♊ 9:36 am
New Moon 1:39 pm
Color of the Day: Rose
Incense of the Day: Rose

New Moon Divination

On this new moon, light a white candle in a holder on your altar. Relax, center your mind, and breathe deeply. Call on Selene, the Greek goddess of the moon. Imagine a pillar of energy move up from the crown of your head and (even though the new moon is physically invisible) consciously connect with Selene's silvery glow. Feel and sense her cool, radiant light moving down the pillar, filling your entire body, and extending outward to form a cocooning sphere of moonlight.

Shuffle an oracle deck of your choice. When you feel ready, draw the top four cards, laying them down from left to right. The first card will provide guidance relevant to the first week of this lunar cycle, the second card to the second week, and so on. When the reading is complete, express gratitude to Selene. As the moon cycle progresses, remember each card as a guiding theme of the week. Be sure to extinguish the candle.

Tess Whitehurst

May 23
Saturday

1st ♊
Color of the Day: Blue
Incense of the Day: Sandalwood

Ramadan ends

Springtime Energy Boost

At this time of year, the weather is usually warm and the world can feel vibrant and alive. Despite the pace of life picking up, we can still feel sluggish. If that is the case, this potion can be a nice energy boost without caffeine. You will need:

- 1 cup peppermint tea
- 1 cup apple juice
- 1 sprig fresh rosemary
- 1 cup club soda or seltzer water

Make the peppermint tea first and allow it to cool completely before combining it with the rest of the ingredients. Once everything is combined and poured into a cup, hold it in your hands and envision it being charged with orange light to fill it with energizing power. As you drink the potion and feel the bubbles, imagine that they are carrying the orange light to every cell in your body, bringing you increased energy.

Michael Furie

May 24
Sunday

1st ♊

☽ v/c 7:09 am

☽ → ♋ 7:09 pm

Color of the Day: Amber

Incense of the Day: Heliotrope

Crafting a Crown of Leaves

To increase your connection to the comforting earth, venture to a park, orchard, or other natural environment. Pick a leaf or two from various trees, whatever you feel called toward. Give thanks to each tree whose leaves you pluck.

After collecting a number of leaves, take a needle and thread and tie them into a circular band. Alternatively, you can get a hole punch and thread the leaves by hand with a cotton string.

In a sacred space, crown yourself with the leaves and envision their natural grounding energy seeping through your head and washing down your entire body. Perform any other earth-based magick or spellcraft at this time.

Be sure to keep your crown in a safe place, and remember to repeat this crowning whenever you are feeling particularly ungrounded in life.

Raven Digitalis

May 25
Monday

1st ♋

Color of the Day: Silver

Incense of the Day: Clary sage

Memorial Day

To Assist the Spirits of Forgotten Warriors

Today in the US, we honor those who have fallen while serving our country as members of the armed forces. In many cultures, it is believed that we can assist those who have moved on by making offerings that can help their afterlives be a bit more comfortable. While we honor our fallen warriors today, it is important to remember that some of them have no one to remember them, and others have no name at all.

Place five bowls of water and five pieces of bread out as an offering today for the forgotten warriors so they, too, can have a more comfortable afterlife. While you do this, say:

Spirits of forgotten warriors, hear my voice and know that you are remembered. Eat of this bread, drink of this water. May you never hunger, may you never thirst!

Leave the offering out until tomorrow morning, then dispose of it.

Devin Hunter

May 26
Tuesday

1st ♋

☽ v/c 9:06 pm

Color of the Day: Scarlet
Incense of the Day: Ginger

Flower Petal Altar Renewal Spell

Spring is a great time to clean up our magickal spaces, and few magickal spaces are more important than our altars. For this spell, you'll need either a bouquet of spring flowers or some flowers picked from your yard or a local park.

Pluck off the petals and let them fall from your hands. Imagine their various energies renewing your altar and your practice. Visualize each color of flower petal with a different property (for example, yellow for creativity, red for passion, blue for emotion, green for stability, orange for health, white for cleanliness, etc.), and let those energies wash over your altar and tools. I also visualize the dropping petals as being symbolic of spring rain and imagine them washing away any negativity or neglect from my altar.

After sprinkling your petals on the altar, leave them there until they have dried out and store for future magickal operations.

Ari & Jason Mankey

May 27
Wednesday

1st ♋

☽ → ♌ 2:33 am

Color of the Day: Brown
Incense of the Day: Honeysuckle

Spell for Justice

On this day in 1679, the Parliament of England passed the Habeas Corpus Act, which strengthened a person's right to challenge unlawful arrest and imprisonment.

There is always an injustice going on in the world, locally and globally. Research a justice issue that matters to you, and figure out how you can make a difference, whether by doing volunteer work, writing a letter, attending a protest, or changing the way you shop.

Take a black stone and dedicate it to Themis, one of the justice goddesses. Pledge to work for justice on this particular issue until it is resolved, and ask for Themis's blessing and guidance.

Leave the stone on your altar as a reminder, and get to work! Once the issue is resolved, give thanks to Themis and bury the stone in the earth.

Cerridwen Iris Shea

May 28
Thursday

1st ♌

☽ v/c 9:30 am

Color of the Day: White
Incense of the Day: Myrrh

To Your health!

Are you a little under the weather? Not feeling like your usual vigorous self? Experiencing some sort of malady? A healing spell will be just the thing.

You'll need a small blue candle in a protective/safe holder (a small Mason jar is ideal) and a small piece of clear quartz crystal.

Light the candle and meditate for a moment on how you currently feel and the changes you are looking for. Take the crystal in your dominant hand and hold it over your heart. Repeat:

Powers of the universe,* I beseech,

Your healing aid I earnestly seek.

May your energies be with me today,

Healing and guiding me on my way.

As this warming candle burns,

May my well-being soon return.

Place the quartz in the candle's wax pool. Allow the candle to burn down safely, extinguishing itself.

*If desired, substitute the name of a favorite deity or guardian for "the universe."

Susan Pesznecker

May 29
Friday

1st ♈ ♌

☽ → ♍ 7:40 am

2nd Quarter 11:30 pm

Color of the Day: Purple
Incense of the Day: Alder

Shavuot (begins at sundown on May 28)

A Safe Travels Charm

In late May, the travel and vacation season begins. This little charm will protect you, your family, and your car this summer. You'll need a square piece of white cloth, garden twine, some crumbled dried mugwort, and salt.

Sprinkle the mugwort and salt in the center of the cloth and tie up the corners with the twine. Sit in your car before traveling while holding the charm and say:

Protect me as I travel near or travel far,

Protect all who travel in this car.

Place the magical bundle in your glove compartment or under a floor mat. If you use it during a long trip, throw it away when you return, as it may have absorbed negative energy. Then make a new one using the same steps.

James Kambos

 May 30
Saturday

2nd ♍

Color of the Day: Black
Incense of the Day: Sage

To Incubate a Dream

This is a simple spell, but one that is very profound. If you want to connect with someone who's no longer in your life, if you need to manifest something, if you hunger to see a plan come to life, here's what to do. You'll need a photo or picture that represents what you want to achieve, a pen, a piece of paper, and an envelope.

Gaze at the image that represents what you hope will happen. Write down your thoughts about this. Keep it simple; just brainstorm your ideas in a few words. Put the image and your writing in the envelope and seal it shut. Place this under your pillow for at least a month, and know that as you sleep, your desire is going out into the cosmos to give you the ideas to make your request come to pass and the energy to breathe life into it.

Charlie Rainbow Wolf

May 31
Sunday

2nd ♏

☽ v/c 5:17 am

☽ → ♎ 10:38 am

Color of the Day: Orange
Incense of the Day: Juniper

A Flowery Ritual

The language of flowers reached its greatest popularity during the reign of Queen Victoria (1837–1901), when social conventions prevented polite people from saying what they really meant. So they used flowers, among other things, to speak for them. Every flower has a meaning. Learn the language of flowers, herbs, and spices. Here are some examples:

- *Dandelion* means "oracle."
- *Ivy* means "fidelity."
- *Jasmine* means "grace and elegance."
- *Iris* means "message."
- *Nasturtium* means "patriotism."
- *Parsley* means "useful knowledge."
- *Cinnamon* means "my fortune is yours."

Gather for a brief ritual in which you and your circle mates give each other flowers whose meanings express your feelings for one another. Announce the meaning of each flower, then invoke Flora (the Roman goddess of flowers) and exchange your flowers:

*These flowers, sweet tokens
of friendship we share,*

*Our circle, the ritual
space in our care—*

*We're sisters and brothers,
all circling today,*

*We're friends here working
or in sacred play.*

So mote it be!

Barbara Ardinger

June

The month of June is a time that inspires warmth, love, passion, and deep appreciation of beauty. Agricultural festivals in old Europe acknowledge and celebrate the many flowers and fruits that become abundant at this time. It is no coincidence that these plants—such as roses, raspberries, strawberries, wildflowers, and those that feature red or pink flowers or fruit—are associated with the planet Venus and the goddess Aphrodite. June is also the traditional month for weddings, and the term *honeymoon* refers to the beverage mead, made from fermented honey, that was traditionally given to the bride and groom as an aphrodisiac.

June brings the start of summer, and for thousands of years the summer solstice has been a prominent festival in many cultures. This celestial festival signifies the beginning of warm weather and abundant growth yet also reminds us of its opposite calendar festival: the winter solstice. All hail the Holly King! Spells done in June are often connected to love, romance, growth, health, and abundance.

Peg Aloi

 June 1
Monday

2nd ♎

Color of the Day: Lavender
Incense of the Day: Rosemary

Planting Good health

The Roman goddess Carna celebrates her festival on this day. She is the goddess of health and protects the vital organs. Offerings made to her were beans and bacon, as the ancient Romans thought that these items promoted good health. She is the goddess to call on if someone is ill.

On a slip of paper, write the name of the individual for whom you are making your petition. Wrap the paper into the shape of a bean. Take this "bean" and plant it outside with other beans or a small piece of bacon. Carna will provide strength to the individual.

Charlynn Walls

June 2
Tuesday

2nd ♎

☽ v/c 6:40 am
☽ → ♏ 12:06 pm

Color of the Day: Red
Incense of the Day: Cedar

The Strength of Family

Use this simple charm to honor and preserve your family's bond. You'll need scissors, a variety of colored construction paper, and colored pens. You might also want to include small stickers, glitter, or anything else you might use to adorn a paper chain. Before beginning, bless the materials with these words:

Link by link, a chain is forged,

Our family's love is its own reward.

Gather the family together around a worktable in a much-used family space. Cut the construction paper into 8 x 1-inch strips. Each family member writes family memories on the links or otherwise decorates them. (For extra magic, work with sigils, runes, and the like.)

Stapled together, the links become a chain, and when the chain's ends are connected, a strong circle is formed.

Display this in your home, or perhaps save it for December's Yule tree. When you pause in front of it, say:

> Our family chain is brilliant and strong,
>
> Our love and pride will be ever-long.

Susan Pesznecker

June 3
Wednesday

2nd ♏

Color of the Day: White
Incense of the Day: Lilac

Empress Empowerment Spell

The Empress card in the Major Arcana of the Tarot reminds us to hold onto our sovereignty. If we yield our power too much to others, we can lose it. Far too often, we're not even aware that we're doing it!

Pull the Empress card from your deck and place it in front of you. Next shuffle the cards and pull three more, placing one to the lower left of the Empress, the second to the lower right, and the third directly below.

The card on the left signifies what or who may be draining you. The card on the right suggests what you need to focus on more in order to stop or prevent that loss. The last card in the center gives the potential outcome of your situation and additional guidance for you.

Laura Tempest Zakroff

June 4
Thursday

2nd ♏

☽ v/c 7:36 am

☽ → ♐ 1:17 pm

Color of the Day: Purple
Incense of the Day: Mulberry

Protecting Our Sacred National Spaces

For the past four years, our national parks, our waters, even the air we breathe have been in peril as protective measures have been erased from our laws. What will remain for future generations? Is our nation turning into a dystopia? It's time to do both practical work and protective spellwork.

First, we can donate to organizations like the Sierra Club, Greenpeace, and Friends of the Earth. Second, we can do volunteer work with local environmental groups. Third, we can work at our altars. If enough of us take action, the energy can build into a critical mass that will lead to positive change.

Begin by laying Tarot cards III (the Empress) and IV (the Emperor) in the center of your altar. Then visualize cards zero (the Fool) and I (the Magician) having a little meeting. Set the Fool and the Magician at the sides of the Empress and the Emperor. Visualize them making plans to protect the land, water, and air.

Barbara Ardinger

 **June 5**
Friday

2nd ♐

☽ Full Moon 3:12 pm

Color of the Day: Rose
Incense of the Day: Yarrow

Lunar Eclipse

Illuminate Your Path

The seeds of intention planted at the new moon are ready for harvest as the moon hangs full in the sky, and this harvesting is supported by taking real-world action. While we might never be privy to our entire life's path in advance, the light of the full moon illuminates our next steps, guiding our actions to best effect. To tap into this guidance, recite the following under the light of the full moon. You can also brew a cup of your favorite tea and allow the moon's reflection to play on the surface, infusing the tea with its energy. Enjoy your magical brew as you perform the spell. Say:

On this eve of full moon light,

My path's revealed and shining bright.

Guide my actions, step by step,

And my highest goals shall all be met.

Spend some time in meditation, journaling any insights that arise. The next morning, take your first action step to reap your full moon harvest.

Melissa Tipton

June 6
Saturday

3rd ♐

☽ v/c 12:10 am

☽ → ♑ 3:44 pm

Color of the Day: Gray
Incense of the Day: Patchouli

Blessing the Rice or Seeds

June is still a traditional time for people to get married, and throwing rice at the couple was once a wedding staple. The practice is still performed on occasion, though throwing bird-seed has gained popularity. In either case, once all of those little baggies are bundled with rice or seeds, they can be charged with the magic of fertility and prosperity, which is what they are sup-posed to symbolize.

When the bundles are created, they are usually gathered together in a basket, and this is where they can be blessed. Holding your hands over the basket, visualize pure white light streaming into the basket, bathing the bundles in magical power, and say:

Delicate bundles, you will be;
talismans of prosperity; bringing
fortune wherever you land;
future blessings close at hand.

Michael Furie

June 7
Sunday

3rd ♑

Color of the Day: Yellow
Incense of the Day: Frankincense

Understanding Life's Lessons Spell

For this spell, you'll need a white candle, a small round piece of mirror, and a bowl of water. Place the mirror in the bowl of water, face up. Carefully light the candle and hold it so the wax drips onto the surface of the water, allowing yourself to go into a light trance. Ponder your question while chanting:

I am open to learning the truth.

I am brave and I am wise.

Lord and Lady, help me to know

So in truth and in love, I can rise!

Let the chant fall off as your trance deepens and the energy flows into the wax and water.

When you're ready, place the candle beside the bowl again, and see what you can read in the wax. Don't worry if no messages come immediately—sometimes it takes a few days for things to fall into place. Remember that messages can come in many forms. Know that clarity will come, and be blessed.

Thuri Calafia

June 8
Monday

3rd ♑

☽ v/c 2:06 pm

☽ → ♒ 8:54 pm

Color of the Day: White
Incense of the Day: Narcissus

World Oceans Day

Sedna is the Inuit goddess of the deep waters and the mother of all creatures of the sea. Appropriately, she must be treated with respect or she will stop providing her vital nourishment to the human race.

Today, create an altar to Sedna. Add seashells if you have them, water in a chalice or glass, and perhaps a blue candle or two in a holder. Sit in front of the altar, light the candle, and relax. Close your eyes and inwardly journey below the waves to the ocean's deepest depths. Make contact with Sedna. Speak gently and lovingly to her. Offer her a pearlescent comb to smooth her tangled hair. Then listen deeply to her counsel: she will share simple ways that you can support the ocean's wellness. Thank her and then return from your meditation. Jot down the guidance you received, as well as any additional ideas you have for how you can personally help heal and protect our world's ocean realms. Extinguish the candle.

Tess Whitehurst

 **June 9**
Tuesday

3rd ♒

Color of the Day: Maroon
Incense of the Day: Basil

Strawberry heart Spell

What makes your heart feel full? Is it music? Meaningful communication? Helping others? Whatever it is, a full heart is a wonderful feeling that tends to be contagious.

Strawberries are perfect representations of the heart, some of them even literally looking like one. For this spell, you'll need a pink candle and a pint of fresh strawberries. Carve or write the words *Full Heart* on the candle.

Arrange the strawberries in the shape of a heart on your altar, with the candle in the center. Light the candle in a holder, and imagine its warmth and glow filling up your heart. Imagine it spreading and permeating the strawberries around it, filling them with this wonderful joyous feeling.

Let the candle burn out. Share the empowered strawberries—and their good feelings—with others to fill the hearts of those around you.

Kate Freuler

June 10
Wednesday

3rd ♒

☽ v/c 10:35 am

Color of the Day: Brown
Incense of the Day: Marjoram

A Daisy Love Spell

Daisies are in bloom now and are one of the strongest love-attracting flowers in existence. For this love spell, you'll need two daisies with long stems, a vase filled with water, and a red candle in a holder. The daisies may be wild, from your garden, or from a florist.

Light the candle and think about the type of person you want to attract. But don't think of a specific person. Next, begin to braid or twist the daisy stems together. As you do, say:

Daisies, flowers of love,

Bring me the romance I'm thinking of.

Hold the daisies to your heart, then place them in the vase. Each day for three days, light the candle, sit before the daisies, and repeat the charm. When the daisies fade, compost them. Extinguish the candle after each use. (You may also use it for other love spells.) Repeat the spell if necessary.

James Kambos

NOTES:

June 11
Thursday

3rd ♒

☽ → ♓ 5:32 am

Color of the Day: Green
Incense of the Day: Jasmine

The Traveling Bucket List

The sun is currently in the sign of Gemini, which is ruled by Mercury, the planet known to rule communication, travel, and swift acts of magick. Much of this is due to Mercury's position as the closest planet to our sun; its quick movement ushers cosmic energy at a fast pace.

Utilize this fast-paced cosmic energy when focusing on goals to travel around the country or world by gathering a number of postcards. These postcards should represent the state, province, or country in which you reside.

Consider the different parts of the world where you wish to travel in your lifetime. Research the addresses of different hotels in each area, and address a postcard to one in each place. Draw the symbols for Mercury (☿) and Gemini (♊) on each postcard, along with the words *Thanks for the great stay!* or something similar. Add the appropriate postage stamp(s) to each envelope, but do not include a return address.

Then affix a small piece of your hair to the sticky part of the postage stamp; don't worry, it won't look suspicious! This will link you to the city. Put the postcards in a public mailbox, along with a loud *See you soon! So mote it be.*

Raven Digitalis

June 12
Friday

3rd ♓

Color of the Day: Coral
Incense of the Day: Cypress

To Know the Truth

It's amazing how many variations of the truth there are when more than one person is involved! This spell works with your own integrity so you can determine what your truth is. It can help you know what's right and how to conduct yourself when you're involved in a dilemma or conflict. You'll need a blue candle, a heatproof surface, and a handful of fresh or dried thyme.

Light the candle on the heatproof surface, and let the wax drip down onto the thyme. As you do this, imagine that droplets of truth are falling around you so you can see clearly through cloudy situations and present yourself as receptive and confident as you work through what needs to be done. Pinch out the candle, and when the wax has cooled, wrap up the thyme in the blue paper, and bury it in the soil where it won't be disturbed.

Charlie Rainbow Wolf

NOTES:

June 13
Saturday

3rd ♓
4th Quarter 2:24 am
☽ v/c 8:45 am
☽ → ♈ 5:03 pm

Color of the Day: Black
Incense of the Day: Ivy

honey harmony Spell

Saturn entered the sign of Aquarius recently, which means that for the next 2.5 years, we will be working on improving our ability to be heard and feel understood. We can cast this spell to bring a little harmony to this placement!

Gather these items:

• Honey

• A plate

• A bowl

• About 12 ounces of fresh water in a glass

Using the honey, draw the astrological glyphs of both Saturn (♄) and Aquarius (♒) on the plate. Position the plate over the bowl, then slowly pour the water from the glass over the glyphs, tilting the plate slightly so the water runs off into the bowl. While you do this, say:

Saturn and Aquarius, my two friends, together you dance and bring good ends!

Deliver the blessings and hold the profane, with your partnership I have much to gain!

Once this is done, drink the honey water and immediately say:

With your partnership, I have much to gain! So must it be!

Devin hunter

June 14
Sunday

4th ♈

Color of the Day: Gold
Incense of the Day: Marigold

Flag Day

Tarot Symbol Spell

Today is Flag Day in the US. Symbols such as flags and the tarot have real power, and it's a power we can tap into easily. Even the simple act of looking at a well-established symbol can have a transformative effect.

Go through your favorite tarot or oracle deck and select the card whose energy you'd most like to bring into your life. Place it upon the pentacle on your altar and then repeat the following exercise over the next thirty days.

In the morning or just before bed, look at your card and envision its image life-size and in front of you. When you have the vision well established, step into the image from the card, and absorb whatever energy you feel and find there. As you practice this exercise, you'll feel more and more energy and the power of the card will begin to resonate within you, bringing about the changes you want.

Ari & Jason Mankey

June 15
Monday

4th ♈
☽ v/c 8:49 pm

Color of the Day: Gray
Incense of the Day: Lily

Pan Blessing

Summer is an ideal time to reconnect with our bodies and the world around us, reminding us of the miracle of being alive on earth. Approached respectfully, the Greek god Pan is an ideal spirit to connect with to aid us.

Take a moment to step out into the world and put your feet into some grass or earth. Breathe deeply and say:

Blessed be, Pan, Lord of the Between!

Hear me, Horned One,
from forest unseen!

Earthly being, all living
things sing of you.

Remind me, great god, to
my own body be true!

Every tree and leaf, every
stem and flower,

As I touch this earth, I feel your power.

Take another deep breath, then place a hand over your heart, close your eyes, and listen to the world around you for a few minutes. Leave a small offering before going on your way if you can.

Laura Tempest Zakroff

June 16
Tuesday

4th ♈

☽ → ♉ 5:35 am

Color of the Day: White
Incense of the Day: Geranium

I Wish I May

We all have wishes. Wouldn't it be great if we could bring them to fruition? Well, today is Wish Fulfillment Day! Working for the things that we really want takes some courage, so you can tap into the energy of Tuesday and Mars to help you succeed.

One easy way to make a wish is to find a dandelion that has gone to seed, then think of your wish and blow the seeds into the air to carry the wish into the world. If a dandelion is not readily available, you can always use a bottle of bubbles. The process is the same. Just blow the bubbles into the air as you concentrate on your wish!

Charlynn Walls

June 17
Wednesday

4th ♉

Color of the Day: Yellow
Incense of the Day: Bay laurel

Just Rest

We underestimate the power of rest. A short period of relaxation can revitalize us for hours.

Call on Pasithea for this spell. She was one of the Greek Charities and the wife of Hypnos, the god of sleep. Pasithea is a goddess of water, charisma, fate, meditation, and rest/relaxation.

Go where you will be undisturbed for at least twenty minutes. Turn off the lights. Play soothing music or light a scented candle or incense. Or have silence.

Ask Pasithea for her blessing. Spend twenty minutes in either Legs Up the Wall pose or Savasana (Corpse) pose.

When you are finished, pour out a liquid libation and thank Pasithea.

Do this whenever you need to revitalize. Even better, turn this into a daily ritual.

Cerridwen Iris Shea

June 18
Thursday

4th ♉

☽ v/c 8:02 am

☽ → ♊ 5:00 pm

Color of the Day: Crimson
Incense of the Day: Nutmeg

Elemental Tarot

Separate out the suits of your favorite tarot deck to create four piles:

Pentacles—Earth

Swords—Air

Wands—Fire

Cups—Water

Alternately, use whichever elemental associations work best for you.

Before shuffling each pile, close your eyes and ask how best to work with each element in regard to your question/situation, then draw a card. For this reading, think of upright and reversed cards as turning the volume either up (upright) or down (reversed) in regard to a particular energetic expression. For example, if you interpret the Two of Pentacles as balance in earth matters, then upright could suggest a need for more balance, while reversed could indicate the benefit of shaking things up. Weave together the messages of all four cards to get full-spectrum guidance on how best to approach your current situation.

Optional: Draw a major arcana card to explore what life lesson this experience is helping you to learn.

Melissa Tipton

June 19
Friday

4th ♊

Color of the Day: Pink
Incense of the Day: Mint

A Self-Blessing

Maybe today is one of those gloomy days and you don't feel so good. Or maybe it's a triumphant day and you want to thank the whole world for the successes of your life.

Put on your favorite piece of jewelry. Cast your circle, alone or with your community, and light candles of your favorite colors. Going deosil (clockwise) around the circle, bless yourselves:

I bless myself

And everything that makes the circle of my life.

I bless myself

And my past, which has made me what I am today.

I bless who I am today,

For this is how I am in the world.

Who I am today pulls me out of the past and thrusts me into the future.

I bless myself

And my uncertainties, my potentialities, my future,

All that leads me toward what I can be.

I bless and give thanks for every day of my life.

Barbara Ardinger

June 20
Saturday

4th ♊

☉ → ♋ 5:44 pm

☽ v/c 5:48 pm

Color of the Day: Indigo
Incense of the Day: Sandalwood

Litha – Summer Solstice

All hail the Sun!

The summer solstice is the year's longest day, when we celebrate light and life and steel ourselves for the return of the dark half. In agricultural terms, it also represents the arrival of summer and the growing season.

Rise early in the morning and enjoy a feast of sunny-side-up eggs—powerful little solar symbols. Dress in fiery colors of orange, red, and sun-gold. Throughout the day, be aware of what is growing around you, and feast abundantly on summer's first fruits and vegetables. A quiche (round like the sun) is a terrific way to celebrate summer's gifts. Be outdoors as much as possible.

In the evening, kindle fire, whether a fire pit in your yard or a candle in the living room. Reflect on the sun's gifts of light and life, intoning:

Thanks for gifts of summer sun,
abundant food and golden light.
Feed our bodies and our souls, and
guide us through the coming night.

Susan Pesznecker

☽★ **June 21**
Sunday

4th ♊

☽ → ♋ 2:02 am

New Moon 2:41 am

Color of the Day: Orange
Incense of the Day: Eucalyptus

Father's Day – Solar Eclipse

To Face Your Shadow Self

It's eclipse day and a great time to deal with your less desirable habits. Everyone has them. They're nothing to be ashamed of, but you can't let them rule you. You'll need a piece of chalk, a piece of black paper, a piece of white paper, and some string.

Using the chalk, write on the black paper one thing you wish to change about yourself, something that you've kept hidden but really wish to work on. You can't fix it if it stays buried. You don't have to broadcast it, but you do have to name and claim it.

Now put the white paper over what you've just written, and rub, transferring the writing. Next, fold the white paper four times, with the writing on the outside of the paper. Tie this closed with the string, and put it on a windowsill to bring light and change into that area of your life.

Charlie Rainbow Wolf

June 22
Monday

1st ♋

Color of the Day: Silver
Incense of the Day: Neroli

Creating Change Spell

For this spell, you'll need a piece of paper and a pen. Divide the paper vertically into two columns.

In the left column, write down the thing you wish to change (for example, "I wish to become more physically fit."). In the right column, write down the steps you need to take to make this change (focusing on your favorite forms of exercise, or taking a yoga class).

Finally, take a small blade or wooden pick and inscribe a candle of the color most appropriate to your goal with an affirmation of the change (such as "I am fit!" or "I am filled with energy and vibrance!").

Light the candle for a few minutes each evening while focusing on the new you, until the full moon. Restate your affirmations whenever you feel tempted to give your energy to fighting the old instead of building the new.

Thuri Calafia

June 23
Tuesday

1st ♋

☽ v/c 3:20 am
☽ → ♌ 8:33 am

Color of the Day: Scarlet
Incense of the Day: Ginger

Maple Leaf Kitchen Spell

Maple trees and their leaves are associated with prosperity and abundance, probably due to the fact that they produce edible maple syrup, which was once used as currency in trade. Here is an easy-to-make charm to attract abundance to your kitchen.

Gather these materials:

- Olive oil (or essential oil of your choice; cinnamon and clove are both associated with prosperity)

- The biggest, greenest maple leaf you can find

Dip your finger in the oil and draw a circle on the leaf, saying:

By sacred circle and bountiful maple,

Abundance and joy will enter here.

Hide the maple leaf somewhere in your kitchen—the center of food, plenty, and wealth—where it will be undisturbed for several months. Later in the year, retrieve the leaf. It will be dried and crumbly. You can grind it and add it to prosperity incense or herb mixtures.

Kate Freuler

June 24
Wednesday

1st ♈ ♌

☽ v/c 1:34 am

Color of the Day: Topaz
Incense of the Day: Lavender

Mint Purification Spell

This spell uses mint (spearmint or peppermint), which should be at its peak about now in the garden, to clear away negative energy hanging around your home. If you don't have mint growing, you can usually find it in the produce section of your super-market. You'll need three stems of mint to use as a "sprinkler" and a dish of salt water.

Stir the salt water three times clockwise using the mint stems. Stir until the salt is dissolved. Then take the dish of salt water and the mint to each exterior door of your home and, using the mint, sprinkle the salt water at each entrance and say:

All negativity, leave this space.

May peace return to this place.

When done, discard the mint and pour the salt water outside away from your home. Use this spell after an argument or after a curmudgeon has left your home.

James Kambos

June 25
Thursday

1st ♈ ♌

☽ → ♍ 1:05 pm

Color of the Day: Turquoise
Incense of the Day: Clove

Magical Seasoning Blend

One of the staples in my kitchen is a blend of herbs usually called "Italian seasoning." It's a great addition not only to Italian dishes but also to soups, sauces, and stews of all kinds, but it can also have magical benefits. I prefer to make and empower my own mixture.

You can mix the ingredients listed below in a bowl and then empower the combined herbs. Each of the herbs is attuned to love, protection, and healing magic, so they can be charged with the general intention "to be an aid to all that is correct and beneficial to whoever consumes them" as you envision the mixture glowing with white light.

I use these herbs in my recipe:

- 1 tablespoon each of basil and oregano

- 2 teaspoons each of rosemary (ground) and thyme

- A pinch of garlic powder

This can be bottled and used whenever a dash of flavorful magic is needed.

Michael Furie

June 26
Friday

1st ♍

Color of the Day: White
Incense of the Day: Rose

Lavender Rest Spell

It's okay to take time for self-care, and with the moon in Virgo today, we are all being asked to make sure we are getting enough rest. This isn't always easy to do, so sometimes we need to make the most of what sleep or relaxation we can muster. Cast this spell on yourself to help take full advantage of your downtime. You will need a cotton ball and some lavender essential oil (or some chamomile essential oil, if you are allergic to lavender).

Five to ten minutes prior to sleep or relaxation, dab three drops of the essential oil onto the cotton ball, then apply directly to the bottoms of your feet. As you do this, say:

Rest is mine, decreed divine,
my body is a sacred shrine.

Rest is mine, decreed divine,
my mind and body now align.

Rest is mine, decreed divine,
a place for my soul to shine!

Take a few deep breaths, then begin your "me time."

Devin Hunter

June 27
Saturday

1st ♍

☽ v/c 4:02 pm
☽ → ♎ 4:16 pm

Color of the Day: Blue
Incense of the Day: Magnolia

Cats: Our Magickal Allies

It's a fact of life that most Witches love animals—especially cats! Here's a little spell for our feline companions.

It's common knowledge that animal overpopulation is a widespread global problem. This is why we choose to get our pets spayed and neutered. Many cats and dogs (as well as other animals) are in great need of loving homes.

Research the ancient Egyptian goddess Bast (Bastet), and ensure that you have a representation of her, even if it's just a printed or hand-drawn image on a sheet of paper. Call to Bast in a manner that you see fit. Burn some natural incense and offer some catnip at her feet. Thank her for her protective and nurturing qualities, and spend some time in meditation.

Take eight small pieces of paper (many cats have eight nipples) and draw a small picture of Bast on each—

it doesn't have to be perfect. Dedicate the pages in her honor, sprinkle some of the offered catnip on each one, then fold each paper a couple times to secure the catnip within it. Take these blessed charms to your local animal shelters. When visiting the cats, secretly leave them throughout the shelter, with a prayer (that you simply whisper or think) for the beloved felines to find loving homes.

Raven Digitalis

June 28
Sunday

1st ♎

2nd Quarter 4:16 am

Color of the Day: Amber
Incense of the Day: Almond

Balance Spell

Today, conditions are perfect to work magic for holistic balance in all life areas. First, pull the Temperance card from a tarot deck of your choice. Place it on your altar. Also light a stick of cedar incense, or diffuse essential oil of cedar. Breathe deeply and relax. Gaze at the image on the card, and come into resonance with its harmonizing vibration. Place your attention on your breath: notice how the in-breath and out-breath perfectly balance themselves when you allow air to naturally flow in and out of your lungs.

Close your eyes. Visualize, imagine, and feel that you are the figure on your Temperance card. Ask yourself: *What needs to come into greater balance in my life? What simple steps can I take today to initiate these positive changes?* Once you receive the clear guidance you seek, open your eyes and write down the messages you received.

Tess Whitehurst

June 29
Monday

2nd ♎

☽ v/c 9:02 am

☽ → ♏ 6:48 pm

Color of the Day: Ivory
Incense of the Day: Hyssop

Garden Joy Spell

The gardens are beautiful now! What a wonderful time to enjoy them. If you have your own garden, be it a traditional one or a container garden, spend some time weeding, trimming, arranging, and giving your plants love and attention. Replant in decorative pots, add sparkly stakes, or build a fairy garden. Talk or sing to your plants, telling them how much you appreciate them.

When you've put in some work, sit down among your tended plants and meditate. Feel the sun on your skin and enjoy the scent of grass and blooms and herbs. Let the joy of growth refresh your spirit.

If you don't have a garden, visit one. Go to a local park or botanical garden, a historic house/garden, or even a garden store. Walk among the plants. Learn their names. Breathe in their scents. Let their energy fill you with pleasure.

Cerridwen Iris Shea

 # June 30
Tuesday

2nd ♏

Color of the Day: Gray
Incense of the Day: Ylang-ylang

Throw the Potato Away Spell

Try as we might, none of us are probably ever going to be universally loved. There's always that one person out there who might be jealous of our accomplishments or simply likes to cause trouble. When those types of folks won't leave you alone, it's time for a magickal remedy. All this spell requires is a small potato, a writing instrument, and a body of water.

Start by writing the name of the person bothering you on your potato. You can do this with a magickal tool or even a ballpoint pen! Surround their name with thoughts like *leave me alone*, *go away*, *bother someone else*, and *with harm to none*. (You want them gone, but there's no reason to hurt them.)

When you're done writing on your potato, throw it into the ocean, a river, or a lake, visualizing that person flying out of your life.

Ari & Jason Mankey

July

In 46 BCE, when Julius Caesar decided to reform the Roman lunar calendar, the names of the months were numbers. He moved the first of the year back to January, and, being the egoist he was, he renamed the fifth month (the month of his birth) for himself: Iulius (Julius, today's July). He also gave it a thirty-first day. (Then he named the next month after his heir, Augustus.)

July (the month of my birth, too) is high summer. In many places, it's the hottest month of the year. It's the month in which everything blooms until the heat of the sun makes flowers—and people—wilt and nearly melt.

What do I remember from my childhood Julys? Rereading my favorite books. Dragging the big old washtub out on the side lawn, filling it with cold water, and splashing all afternoon. Helping my father tend his flowers—roses, columbines, tulips, and hydrangeas. Climbing to the very top of our neighbor's huge weeping willow tree. Chasing fireflies before bedtime and putting them in jars to glitter and wink throughout the night. Sleeping in the screened porch with all the windows open to catch every possible breeze. What are your favorite July memories?

Barbara Ardinger

July 1
Wednesday

2nd ♏

☽ v/c 9:20 pm

☽ → ♐ 9:21 pm

Color of the Day: Brown
Incense of the Day: Marjoram

Canada Day

Confidence Candle

Self-confidence is essential to a happy life, and we can always use more of it. You can make a candle to boost your confidence.

You'll need:

- A light-colored pillar candle and holder

- A sharp nail, skewer, or large metal darning needle

- A fine-tipped permanent marker

- A candle extinguisher

Make a quick list of things that make you feel confident, your successes, or times you've felt extra-capable. Using your sharp tool, inscribe these into the candle, filling the space from top to bottom. Once you're done, use the marker to fill in the etchings, making them stand out.

Place the candle in a holder on your altar and light it. Intone:

With the rising candle flame, faith in myself is deeply ingrained.

Meditate on your confidence! Then extinguish the flame, saying:

As I put the candle out, so I extinguish worry and doubt.

Use your candle whenever you need a boost of confidence.

Susan Pesznecker

July 2
Thursday

2nd ♐

Color of the Day: Green
Incense of the Day: Balsam

A Spell to Increase Self-Love

Let's be honest: we all struggle with self-esteem from time to time. Witches, Wiccans, Pagans, and other metaphysical folk tend to be quite sensitive to energies—and most certainly to the emotional energies of others. Even some of the least empathic people among us can sometimes carry the weight of others' judgments for years or even a lifetime, sometimes unconsciously!

As difficult and even painful as it can be, we must all learn to love ourselves for who we are. There is always room for self-improvement, but we as magickal workers have a responsibility to care for ourselves and inspire this same care in others.

Get a small, fancy piece of paper that you can easily carry in your wallet or bag after the spell has been cast. In a sacred space (whether at home at your altar or in a spot in nature), carefully draw one small drop of blood from your body (such as with a sterile needle) and place it in the middle of the paper. Strongly press this droplet with the ring finger of your right hand, leaving your fingerprint in the center.

Around the fingerprint, draw images of smiley faces, hearts, and other symbols and words that you associate with love. Speak these words three times:

> Love above, love below, love
> within, and love without.
> (Your name), I love you.

Keep this spell in your wallet, bag, pocket, car, or otherwise on your person whenever possible.

Raven Digitalis

 July 3
Friday

2nd ♐

☽ v/c 9:06 am

Color of the Day: Purple
Incense of the Day: Violet

A Rain Blessing

We complain about rain, but we need it to survive. During July's heat, it's a good time to show your appreciation for rain by performing a rain blessing. You'll need a rainy day and your cauldron.

When rain is forecast, place your cauldron outdoors in a safe place. When the rain is done, sit before your cauldron, preferably outside. Anoint your forehead with a drop of the rainwater. Then hold your hands over the cauldron and say this blessing:

Sweet rain, thank you for
falling, each and every drop.

Sweet rain, thank you for watering
the earth and every crop.

When done, you may use the rainwater to cleanse your ritual tools. End by pouring the remaining rainwater onto a favorite plant.

James Kambos

July 4
Saturday

2nd ♐

☽ → ♑ 12:48 am

Color of the Day: Blue
Incense of the Day: Pine

Independence Day

Personal Independence Day Spell

In the United States, it's Independence Day and a perfect time to declare your personal independence from something that is holding you back.

Gather these supplies:

• White paper

• A red pen

• A white candle in a holder

• Matches or a lighter

• A blue ceramic dish

Pick one thing in your life from which you wish to declare your independence. Write it on the paper in red ink.

Light the candle, saying:

This flame represents the
spark of liberty.

Carefully touch the paper to the flame and say:

I declare my independence
from (what's written).

Drop the paper into the dish and watch it burn to ash. Scatter to the winds. Let the candle burn down on its own if possible.

Repeat the declaration if you feel pulled back into a negative pattern.

Cerridwen Iris Shea

 July 5
Sunday

2nd ♑
Full Moon 12:44 am

Color of the Day: Gold
Incense of the Day: Juniper

Lunar Eclipse

Balancing Act

The energies of the full moon are at the forefront today. It is also a Sunday, which means that you can tap into the energies of the sun. Today you can work to bring balance into any aspect of your life.

You will want to call on the moon and sun to help you in this endeavor while working to literally balance some object. It could be stacking stones or balancing a pen on your forefinger. While you are working to bring about a physical manifestation of your desire, say:

*Help me find my balance today, as
the moon and sun both hold sway.*

Repeat this verse until you are able to balance the object you are working with.

Charlynn Walls

 July 6
Monday

3rd ♑

☽ v/c 5:35 am

☽ → ♒ 6:08 am

Color of the Day: Silver
Incense of the Day: Clary sage

Seashell Secrets

There's a superstition that if you hold a conch shell to your ear, you will hear the ocean. Some even say it can help you hear the voice of divinity or receive guidance from water spirits.

Make this charm if you feel lost and in need of direction. This spell can be done with any fresh or saltwater shell that appeals to you. It doesn't have to be an actual conch shell. It just needs to be small enough to carry with you.

After dark, place your shell in a jar of water. Water represents intuition and psychic awareness. Let the shell absorb the intuitive energy of the water overnight. In the morning, gaze at the shell in the water and say:

Intuition in my ear,

Tell me what I need to hear.

Carry the shell with you until you receive the guidance or omen you desire. Keep your ears, eyes, and other senses open!

Kate Freuler

July 7
Tuesday

3rd ♒

☽ v/c 12:37 am

Color of the Day: Black
Incense of the Day: Cinnamon

Salt of the Earth

For this spell, you'll need two tablespoons of Epsom salt and a gallon of water. Place your hands over the salt and say:

I call on the spirit of salt to bring nourishment and balance to my garden. Thank you, salt!

Keep your hands over the salt, allowing energy to flow for a few moments. Then place your hands over the water and say:

I call on the element of water to bring health and blessings to my garden. Thank you, water!

Allow energy to flow from your hands for a few moments, then add the salt to the water and shake or stir to dissolve.

Use the mixture to water your plants. It's especially good for flowering plants, such as roses and rhododendrons, and fruits and vegetables, such as tomatoes, peppers, and citrus trees, boosting flavor, output, and overall plant health.

Melissa Tipton

 July 8
Wednesday

3rd ≈≈

☽ → ♓ 2:13 pm

Color of the Day: Yellow
Incense of the Day: Honeysuckle

Magnetic Travel Spell

Take two magnets and bless them, saying:

These two magnets together are bound,

May all return to me safe and sound.

Keep one magnet in your pocket and place the other one in your travel bag. They will continually attract each other and ensure that your luggage won't be lost or stolen and will return safely to you while traveling. Alternatively, you can travel with one magnet and leave the other at home, ensuring a safe return.

Ari & Jason Mankey

July 9
Thursday

3rd ♓

Color of the Day: Purple
Incense of the Day: Apricot

To Banish What Is No Longer Useful

It doesn't matter whether this is clutter that's messing up your home, emotional baggage that's messing up your life, or a belief system you've outgrown: if it has outlived its purpose, it has to go. You can't open the doors to abundance if they're cluttered with things that are in the way! You'll need a pen and paper, a black candle on a heatproof surface, something to light the candle with, and tweezers.

Write down what you want to be rid of on the paper. Light the candle, and carefully set fire to the paper in the flame. When it has burned down so that it's hard to hold, grab the end of the paper with the tweezers. You have to burn every last scrap of the paper. Pinch out the candle. Sweep up the remains of the paper, and dispose of them off your property.

Charlie Rainbow Wolf

July 10
Friday

3rd ♓

☽ v/c 11:49 pm

Color of the Day: Pink
Incense of the Day: Thyme

Invisibility Spell

Sometimes we just don't want to be seen! While this spell won't work like Harry Potter's invisibility cloak, it can serve well to divert attention away so the person you're avoiding will be, well, avoidable!

For this spell, gather together a pinch of amaranth (love-lies-bleeding), lemon peel, mugwort, and mistletoe. Mix well while chanting:

I am a whisper, like the wind.

I am a spark in earth so deep.

I am flowing, sliding, gossamer silent,

Never to be seen!

When the power peaks, visualize yourself completely invisible wherever you go. Cover the herbs with olive oil and simmer in a double boiler for three and a half hours or in a slow cooker for thirteen hours. Strain off the oil and anoint yourself whenever you wish to be hidden, repeating the chant as needed.

Thuri Calafia

July 11
Saturday

3rd ♓

☽ → ♈ 1:06 am

Color of the Day: Indigo
Incense of the Day: Sage

Seventh Wave Spell

There is much maritime lore about the seventh wave, particularly about it being the largest wave in a group, and the one that hits the shore directly. The next time you find yourself by a body of water, watch the waves as they come in, and you'll start to see the seventh-wave pattern.

Use the power and directness of the wave to call something to you as you watch it come in. Visualizing your goal, say to the waves:

One and two, three and four,
waves crashing upon the shore.

Five and six and seventh wave,
to my door bring what I crave.

Leave a token or drawn symbol of thanks at the shoreline before you go.

Laura Tempest Zakroff

July 12
Sunday

3rd ♈

4th Quarter 7:29 pm

Color of the Day: Yellow
Incense of the Day: Hyacinth

Shielding Spell during Sun in Cancer

With both Mercury and the sun in Cancer now, you may be feeling a little emotional. Cast this spell to strengthen your empathic shields and to help keep your energy stable and grounded during this time. All you need is a small piece of black tourmaline (or your favorite protection stone).

Hold the tourmaline in your dominant hand and make a fist. Lift your fist to your third eye, then move it down to your chest, your belly, and finally both feet. As you do this, imagine a line of white light connecting each of the points on your body, and say:

Stone of strength, lend your might,
shield me from all but light.

Fortify me as I block and defend,
and when I crack, my energy mend!

Keep the stone in your pocket for as long as you need it.

Devin Hunter

July 13
Monday

4th ♈

☽ v/c 11:54 am

☽ → ♉ 1:34 pm

Color of the Day: Lavender
Incense of the Day: Lily

John Dee's Birthday

Elizabethan mathematician, physician, alchemist, theologian, philosopher, astrologer, scholar, and royal advisor John Dee was so masterfully accomplished that it's impossible to describe the scope of his genius here. In addition to his significant contributions to numerous branches of science and history, he (along with his colleague Edward Kelley) spoke with angels and developed a unique magical system featuring ornate sigils and an entire angelic language. And today is his birthday!

To honor John Dee's spirit and celebrate his wisdom, light a white candle and offer him a glass of English wine. Let his memory inspire your studies: magical, spiritual, or secular. Take a moment to note any disciplines you'd like to delve into more thoroughly. Research avenues of learning that match your interests: books, classes, workshops, and course studies. Take at least one concrete step toward your educational goals, even if it's just reserving a book at the library. Be sure to extinguish the candle.

Tess Whitehurst

July 14
Tuesday

4th ♉

Color of the Day: Scarlet
Incense of the Day: Bayberry

Vacation Safety Charm

Since the modern world has become so security-focused, it is ironic that we cannot really make travel safety charms out of herbs without risking creating a big travel hassle in the form of security checks and a whole lot of questions.

Luckily, there is a gemstone that can be protective but also inconspicuous. That stone is malachite. It is a beautiful green stone that has a reputation for being the prime protective gem for travelers. It is becoming more mainstream and can be found in jewelry, which is a great benefit during travel.

To help focus the stone, you can hold it while visualizing a safe journey and say:

Stone of power, protection, and might;
keep me safe the whole way through;
whether on foot, by car, boat, or
flight; keep my course safe and true.

Michael Furie

NOTES:

July 15
Wednesday

4th ♂

☽ v/c 11:21 pm

Color of the Day: White

Incense of the Day: Lilac

Binding Adversity

This spell will rid you of unwanted memories, energies, or other influences. You'll need:

- Black salt
- Small pieces of black crystals
- Fresh or dried herbs for burning (bay laurel, rosemary, thyme)
- A small iron cauldron or dish (or similar device for burning)
- A black ink pen
- White paper
- Black paper
- Black cord or yarn

Cast this spell outside, working on a dark or waning moon between sunset and midnight. Place the salt, crystals, and herbs in the cauldron. Say:

Now the binding begins.

Using the pen and white paper, write down what you wish to bind or remove from your life. Draw a circle around the words. Tear the paper into bits, allowing the bits to fall into the cauldron. Light the cauldron. As the paper bits and herbs burn, intone:

Through blackened fire, may _____ no longer darken my thoughts.

Let the cauldron contents cool, then place on the black paper and roll, burrito-style. Tie with the cord and bury outside. Say:

Now it is done.

                              Susan Pesznecker

July 16
Thursday

4th ♉

☽ → ♊ 1:19 am

Color of the Day: Crimson
Incense of the Day: Mulberry

The Ouroboros

Snakes are some of the oldest creatures, and they have certainly made it into the iconography for many different paths. World Snake Day is celebrated today. This is a perfect time to connect to the ouroboros, which is the symbol depicting a snake swallowing its own tail. This symbol represents the cycle of renewal and infinity.

To connect with the ouroboros, find a comfortable place to sit and meditate. Relax and picture in your mind the serpent circling in on itself. Ask yourself what you need to circle back in on and recreate in your life. Hold that thought in your mind's eye and feel the energy of the snake circling around you and back in on itself. Let the energy build until you are ready to release it into the universe for it to begin working.

Charlynn Walls

 **July 17**
Friday

4th ♊

☽ v/c 5:14 pm

Color of the Day: Coral
Incense of the Day: Yarrow

The Man in the Moon

The moon hasn't always belonged to goddesses. There have also been many lunar gods, whose names you can find online. Perhaps one such god is the Man in the Moon. I know of two songs about him, one by Jerry Herman (in the musical *Mame*) and the other by Bilbo Baggins. And Genghis Khan traced his ancestry back to a moon god.

It's time to make friends with the Man in the Moon. How did he get there? One folktale says that he is a wanderer, doomed to forever circle the earth. He obviously sees a lot. What can he do for us? According to several traditions, he watches over us. Go outside tonight, look up, and speak to him:

Old Man in the Moon, I see you up there

Looking down, watching everywhere.

What do you see

When you look at me?

What advice do you have tonight?

How can I live this life aright?

Barbara Ardinger

July 18
Saturday

4th ♊

☽ → ♋ 10:24 am

Color of the Day: Gray
Incense of the Day: Ivy

Altar Refresh Spell

Even when we use our altar every day and cleanse and consecrate the items for spells and rituals, we often forget to clean the altar.

Today, remove everything from your altar so it is completely bare. Wash and wipe it down. Smudge it with your favorite cleansing scent. Ground and center by standing in front of your altar, using your feet to connect to the stability of the earth beneath the floor. Breathe until you feel the connection. Bless the altar, saying:

Clean slate,

Fresh take,

Blessed fate.

Take a look at each item you removed. Clean and bless each one. Decide what you want to place back on the altar, what needs to be changed/freshened, and what needs to be put away.

When you're finished, light your altar candles and take a few minutes to meditate in your freshened space.

Cerridwen Iris Shea

July 19
Sunday

4th ♋

Color of the Day: Amber
Incense of the Day: Frankincense

Incense Divination

Go outdoors and light a stick of incense. Put it in a holder in front of you and ask:

How will (state the situation) turn out?

As the incense burns, pay attention to which cardinal direction the smoke drifts to most frequently to get your answer.

North = Earth. The answer lies in the material world. The outcome may be more plain and simple than you'd like but is best for everyone.

East = Air. The answer will come to you from another person, a book, or a written message. Beware of misinformation. Listen only to those you trust.

South = Fire. The answer will arrive in a dramatic, transformative way. This may be a blow-up or sudden change. Beware of anger or arguments.

West = Water. The answer will lie in calm emotions and a peaceful resolution. Be sure not to let others sway your decisions.

Kate Freuler

July 20
Monday

4th ♋
New Moon 1:33 pm
☽ v/c 1:55 pm
☽ → ♌ 4:16 pm

Color of the Day: White
Incense of the Day: Narcissus

Dark Moon Scrying

Here is an invocation to harness the energy of the new (or dark) moon for scrying:

Dark moon in bed of starry night,

Shadowy wisdom granting sight.

Lift the veil between the worlds,

So the spirits' path is unfurled.

Hidden knowledge revealed anew,

Safely guided now, give the view!

Laura Tempest Zakroff

July 21
Tuesday

1st ♌
☽ v/c 8:27 pm

Color of the Day: Maroon
Incense of the Day: Cedar

A household Smudging Consecration

Burning sage is a great way to cleanse small amounts of residual negative energy from a space. In many ways, smudging is considered to be an act of energetic neutralization.

To add an extra boost of protection to your home, smudge every room, drawer, and closet of your house. Walk in a deosil (clockwise) fashion in order to accomplish this. Sing a special song or recite an appropriate mantra while doing so.

Afterward, choose four sticks of all-natural incense and do the same thing. This time, however, venture outside your home (or apartment building), and make a full deosil circle around the property. Carefully place a stick of incense near the four corners of the house; ensure that they are secured, and be sure to check them later.

At each quadrant, offer prayers to the Watchtowers, the elements, the cardinal directions, and any local spirits or personal guides with whom you feel a kinship.

Raven Digitalis

 July 22
Wednesday

1st ♌

☉ → ♌ 4:37 am

☽ → ♍ 7:40 pm

Color of the Day: Yellow
Incense of the Day: Bay laurel

Garden Rune Spell

Find several flat stones, preferably from your own yard or neighborhood. Wash them with soap and water, then cleanse them with salted water and the incense of your choice (such as sandalwood or myrrh).

When your stones are clean physically and magickally, paint (or draw with a marker) your favorite runes (or other magickal symbols) on them. We like to do the painting on our house altar for an extra added bit of energy. Choose runes that are associated with fertility, such as Fehu, Uruz, Wunjo, or Jera, and add a protective rune or two, such as Thurisaz or Eihwaz, to keep the squirrels from eating your tomatoes!

When the paint is dry, bury the runes in your garden (or pot, if you have a container gardener). Their energy will act as a magickal fertilizer, adding a little extra zing (and protection) to your garden. You can bury your runes during any moon phase, but full and waxing moons provide the best results.

Ari & Jason Mankey

July 23
Thursday

1st ♍

Color of the Day: Turquoise
Incense of the Day: Myrrh

Wandering Magic

Many of us spend the majority of our time on a schedule that leaves precious little time for meandering and exploring. This spell is ideal for a day off, whether at home or on vacation, to help you break out of patterns that are narrowing your perception of what is possible. I like to hold a bottled drink or a to-go snack in my hands as I say the spell, charging it with my intention. I take the charged food on my adventures to reinforce the magic as I sip or snack. Say:

I open to the magic

That is hidden in all things.

I surrender plans and schedules

On this day of meandering.

*Through doors unknown
and paths untread,*

My soul will guide the way

And lead me like a string of lights

Through a wonder-full, expansive day.

Set out on your adventure and stay curious. Let the magic guide you to unexpected places, people, and situations. Have fun!

Melissa Tipton

July 24
Friday

1st ♈ ♍

☽ v/c 7:08 pm

☽ → ♎ 9:54 pm

Color of the Day: Rose
Incense of the Day: Orchid

Weeding Our Spiritual Landscape Spell

Now, at the height of the summer season, many of us can find ourselves feeling burned-out from having too much to do and too many commitments. This is a spell to bring balance back to our lives.

First, take a black candle and use a small blade or wooden pick to carve it with symbols of all the things you wish to do but have no idea how to make time for. Then take a white candle and carve it with the things you're currently managing. Light both candles and take turns dripping the wax from the black candle onto the white one, and vice versa, while chanting:

Show me where to pull the weed.

Show me where to plant the seed.

Show me where to find the time;

To fly, to soar, to make this mine!

Let the power peak, shooting it into the candles, then place them close together on your altar. Do some wax scrying, if desired, on how the candles melted. Extinguish the candles. Know that the divine is opening up space in your life for all of your most cherished wishes. Blessed be.

Thuri Calafia

July 25
Saturday

1st ♎

Color of the Day: Brown
Incense of the Day: Sandalwood

Messenger Feather

Finding a feather on the ground is a gift from nature. A feather's association with the air element makes it a wonderful all-natural item to include in spells for communication or sending messages. If you have a message or positive feeling you wish to send to someone but you can't see them or contact them in real life, try using this feather spell to get in touch with them subconsciously.

Next time you happen across a feather on the ground, hang onto it. Write the initials of the person you wish to contact on the feather with paint or ink. Cast a circle, if you wish, and sit quietly with the feather in your hand. See the recipient clearly in your mind. Whisper your message to the feather—keep it short and clear.

Go outside and set the feather down. Let it be taken away by the wind. Nature will carry the message to your friend.

Kate Freuler

July 26
Sunday

1st ♎
☽ v/c 9:09 pm

Color of the Day: Orange
Incense of the Day: Almond

To Reconnect with Someone Special

Mercury is finally out of its storm, and things should start moving forward again. To celebrate this, here's a spell to get communication going smoothly again between you and a loved one. You'll need a pen and paper, a needle with yellow thread, and a photo of yourself.

Write your loved one's name on the paper, and draw a circle around it. Thread the needle and sew the person's name to your photo. Communication between the two of you should start to open up shortly, and any misunderstandings you've had can now be laid to rest, even if it's just to give you closure so you can move on.

Charlie Rainbow Wolf

July 27
Monday

1st ♎

☽ → ♏ 12:12 am

2nd Quarter 8:33 am

Color of the Day: Ivory
Incense of the Day: Clary sage

Seven Sleepers

Today, the Catholic Church honors the Seven Sleepers. According to Islamic and Christian legend, the Seven Sleepers were persecuted Christians who escaped martyrdom in a unique way: they went to sleep in a cave near Ephesus and woke up 300 years later, thinking they had slept for merely a single night. (Today in Finland, their slumber is commemorated by the different but derivative holiday National Sleepy Head Day.)

Petition the Seven Sleepers for deep and restful sleep by placing seven cups of chamomile tea on your altar. Then tie the following seven herbs into a bundle with a scrap of cotton, or add them to an eye pillow or drawstring bag: chamomile, passionflower, valerian, lavender, lemon balm, skullcap, and hops. Clear any clutter out of your bedroom, wash your sheets, and make sure the atmosphere is restful and calm. Sleep with the herb bundle near you so you can inhale the scent.

Tess Whitehurst

▽ **July 28**
Tuesday

2nd ♏

Color of the Day: Gray
Incense of the Day: Bayberry

Thank the Great Mother Ritual

In late July the Goddess, or "Great Mother," begins to bless us with the bounty of the land. Take time to thank her with this ritual. The only spell ingredient you'll need is some birdseed or some other small offering.

Sit in a quiet place outside or at your altar and say:

Great Mother,

Thank you for blessing the soil and the seeds.

Great Mother,

Thank you for our food and caring for our needs.

End by scattering the birdseed on the ground near your home if possible. When you can, go to a farmers' market or an orchard and buy some fruits and vegetables to support your local farmers. When you eat them, eat with purpose and think of the words you said honoring the Great Mother.

James Kambos

July 29
Wednesday

2nd ♏

☽ v/c 12:01 am

☽ → ♐ 3:25 am

Color of the Day: Topaz
Incense of the Day: Marjoram

Justice Spell

Mars is in the sign of Aries right now, highlighting our need for justice and fairness in just about every area of our lives. Cast this spell to balance the scales and bring proper order to legal, financial, and health issues in your life.

You will need a block of wood, a black marker, and a hammer. Using the marker, draw a pentacle on one side of the block of wood, and the name of the person you're seeking justice for on the other side. Take your hammer and hold it in your dominant hand, then say:

I declare this hammer Justice!

Then tap both sides of the block, each time demanding that a specific action occur, such as *The judge will overturn the ruling because_____, or They will see the evidence and have no doubt about_____.*

Once you have said your piece, bury the block of wood near your front door to bring about swift change.

Devin Hunter

July 30
Thursday

2nd ♐

☽ v/c 8:08 pm

Color of the Day: White
Incense of the Day: Clove

Online Friends

Many of us have lots of online friends: official Facebook friends, people who tweet, those who perform on YouTube, and even email friends with whom we exchange frequent notes. It's good to have friends, even if they're only words on your phone or faces on your screen. But what if they're not really friends? What if they're spammers or phishers or thieves? It's time to do a protection spell for the benefit of yourself and your true friends.

Lay Tarot cards VIII (Justice, in the French stream) and XI (Strength) on your altar. Lay your devices on the cards. Light red and black candles. Now speak to Justice and Strength:

I call to you to protect me, to secure my devices and my identity, and to bless my true online friends. Great Powers, chase away offenders and thieves of my security online and in person.

Let the candles safely burn down (but not drip on your electronics!). Then give thanks to the Powers.

Barbara Ardinger

July 31
Friday

2nd ♐

☽ → ♑ 7:58 am

Color of the Day: Pink
Incense of the Day: Vanilla

Pre-harvest Cooldown

One of the primary facets of my practice at this time of year is to work sympathetic magic aimed at cooling the heat of the sun so its intensity will not destroy the crops before they can be harvested and also because by this time, the summer heat has more than worn out its welcome.

To work this magic, place an orange or red candle within a cauldron to symbolize the power of the sun. Next, carefully pour water in the cauldron around the candle so it can still burn. Light the candle and allow it to continue to burn down until it reaches the water. As the water overtakes it and it begins to sputter, say:

*Life-giving star of powerful force,
calm the heat, do not destroy.*

*To save the crops, our food source,
balance of water I employ.*

Michael Furie

NOTES:

August

Summer is at its height of power when August rolls in, bringing with it the first of the harvest festivals, Lughnasadh (or Lammas), on the first of the month. Lughnasadh is a festival of strength and abundance, a reflection of August itself. Lugh and the Corn God are highly celebrated during this month and are particularly good to work with in spells or rituals for abundance, prosperity, agriculture, marriage, or strength. The Earth Mother in her many forms is ripening and overflowing with abundance. While we often see the first harvest as being associated with corn, there is much more that has been harvested by this point. We must remember not to overlook anything or take anything for granted in our lives, and the harvest is an excellent reminder of that. It is a time to begin focusing on expressing appreciation and giving thanks for all that we have.

The full moon this month is most often called the Corn Moon, but also goes by the Wyrt Moon, Barley Moon, or Harvest Moon. The stones carnelian, fire agate, cat's eye, and jasper will add extra power to your spells and rituals at this time. Use the herbs chamomile, St. John's wort, bay, angelica, fennel, rue, barley, wheat, marigold, or sunflowers in your spells. The colors for August are yellow, gold, and the rich green of the grass and leaves.

Kerri Connor

August 1
Saturday

2nd ♑

Color of the Day: Blue
Incense of the Day: Rue

Lammas

Reconnection with Self and Patron Spirits

Lammas is the most important day in my personal ritual calendar (the anniversary of my initiation), along with being the first harvest.

Prepare your ritual space, and have offerings of fresh-baked cornbread, grapes, and beer. Cast a circle with your wand, athame, or hand. Start in the north or the east. Use your tool to send out energy, defining the sacred circle you will use, turning clockwise until you end up in the direction in which you began.

Then invite the directions, starting with the direction in which you began casting, moving clockwise. You can use specific attributes for each direction, such as north/earth, east/air, south/fire, and west/water. It can be something as simple as this:

Welcome, spirits of the north, element of earth, to this sacred circle.

Invite Lugh (if appropriate) and your patron deities.

Take time to center and connect with your core as deeply as you can. Thank the deities for their guidance and help during this cycle. Don't ask for anything; just listen.

Offer libations to the deities. Place your hands on the ground, sending any excess energy back into the earth and feeling its stability. Close the circle with the tool you used to cast it, starting in the direction you began (north or east) but moving counterclockwise, thanking each direction for being there and imagining the energy of the circle retracting into the tool.

Write down what you intuited from the spirits, and take the next few weeks to consider, in daily meditations, how to take the actions they advise.

Cerridwen Iris Shea

August 2
Sunday

2nd ♑

☽ v/c 9:59 am

☽ → ♒ 2:11 pm

Color of the Day: Amber
Incense of the Day: Heliotrope

Blessing for a Safe Pregnancy for Pregnant Women

Take a cauldron or bowl (representing the future mother's womb) and fill it with clean water, along with essential oils associated with protection (such as frankincense or cedarwood).

To the water, add the energies of the elements via a symbol or token for each of them (such as air/feather, earth/stone, fire/ash, and water/seashell), along with symbols that to you and the mother are representative of possibility, health, and safety. Finally, add a seed to the bowl (to represent the child). Place the bowl over a picture of the mother-to-be (or if she's with you, have her touch or hold the bowl) and say:

May no harm come to child or mother,

Let this be a time of
magick and wonder.

Mother Goddess, we ask this of thee,

Hear our plea and so mote it be!

Remove the seed from the bowl and give it to the expectant mother. If she lives far away, the seed may be sent to her.

Ari & Jason Mankey

August 3
Monday

2nd ♒

Full Moon 11:59 am

Color of the Day: Gray
Incense of the Day: Rosemary

Break a habit

The Aquarius full moon is perfect for setting in motion positive changes that require a fresh perspective and an improved frame of mind, which includes breaking habits that no longer serve us.

Ideally under the light of the full moon, stand on the earth barefoot. Hold a glass bottle of water in both hands. Relax and center your mind. Get in touch with the energy of the habit you want to break. Feel or sense it as roots, cobwebs, or cords in your aura, attached to the habit. Mentally send this energy out of your body and into the water through your hands. When this feels complete, pour the water out onto the soil, feeling lighter and freer as you do so. Then safely light a stick of palo santo wood, and smudge your body. Feel and sense the smoke balancing, repairing, and recalibrating your energy field. Give thanks to the full moon.

Tess Whitehurst

August 4
Tuesday

3rd ♒

☽ v/c 5:45 pm

☽ → ♓ 10:28 pm

Color of the Day: White
Incense of the Day: Basil

Deep, Bright healing Spell

Sometimes life gives us more than we can handle and we need to take some time to ourselves to relax and heal. Sometimes we can aggravate the situation by doing things that aren't in our best interest (such as sugar bingeing or smoking too much when we're hurting emotionally), and it can be difficult to find the strength to break those bad habits.

For this spell, take a simple clear quartz crystal and program it to help give you strength by reminding you of your self-love and care. Program the crystal by holding it in your left (or most receptive) hand, then focus deeply, visualizing energy flowing from your right hand into the crystal in your left hand. While doing so, say:

Great goddess, make me strong now.

Great god, please make me brave.

Lord and Lady, help me remember

Whose life and love I save.

For I am worth the effort,
For the gods have made me, so
I know that we can heal my life
And together, make me whole!

Keep the crystal on your person and visualize yourself healed and thriving, repeating the chant as necessary.

Thuri Calafia

August 5
Wednesday

3rd ♓

Color of the Day: Yellow
Incense of the Day: Lavender

Your Magic Wand

Today is the first day of the month of Hazel in the Celtic tree calendar. Hazel (or *Coll*, "the life force in you") is associated with springs, wells, wisdom, and divination. It's said that the best magic wands are made of hazel. If you live where hazel trees grow, ask a tree for a slender limb; otherwise, search online and find hazel wands for sale.

Whether you have a fresh limb or an already-made wand, your first task is to cleanse it. Cast your circle and sit inside it for this work. Use smudge to release old vibes from the wand and fresh or bottled water to wash it. Now decorate your wand with paint, beads, ribbons, or whatever you want to make it truly yours. Finally, dedicate your wand to the goddess or god to whom you feel closest. Use the wand the next time you cast a circle.

Barbara Ardinger

August 6
Thursday

3rd ♓

Color of the Day: Turquoise
Incense of the Day: Apricot

Fire Up Your Will

Fire is symbolic of our will: the ability to direct our energy to create desired change. The more focused this energy is, the more potent our efforts will be. This spell will illuminate obstructions to your will and help you transform them with fire.

Light a red candle in a holder and focus on the flame. Hold your hands near the warmth and feel the energy travel up your arms and into your body, suffusing your entire being. Say:

Fire, fire, show me true,

Where my will is thrown askew.

Obstructions I now see most clear,

And the highest good comes into view.

Spend time in meditation, open to thoughts, feelings, and guidance. When you identify an obstacle or distraction, draw in more fire energy and infuse the obstacle, seeing and/or feeling it transform. You might receive guidance for practical changes needed to back up this energetic transformation, so be sure to take appropriate action following the meditation.

Melissa Tipton

August 7
Friday

3rd ♓

☽ v/c 8:53 am

☽ → ♈ 9:05 am

Color of the Day: Purple
Incense of the Day: Violet

Cool Head Spell

There is something about August that makes tempers and troubles rise. Whether because of hot, strong winds or high temperatures, or the gaze of Leo the Lion, August seems to bring an uptick in violence and disagreements. To keep your cool, head to your freezer and grab an ice cube. (You may wish to wrap it up in some cloth or use tongs when you do this spell.)

With the ice cube, draw the shape of a pentagram at each part of the body as named here, saying:

When violence threatens, may my hands work for peace.

When rage consumes, let my heart soothe the burns.

When tempers flare, may my lips speak healing words.

When the heat rises, my mind shall be cool and calm.

If any of the ice remains, allow it to melt in a cup. Then pour it as an offering to a nearby plant.

Laura Tempest Zakroff

August 8
Saturday

3rd ♈

Color of the Day: Black
Incense of the Day: Patchouli

Sacred Waters, Charged Waters

Water is essential to all life and has a regular use in every kind of spellcraft. Collecting sacred or special waters from various locations and charging them before use just adds to their oomph.

Begin by keeping a couple of small bottles or vials tucked into your purse, glove box, backpack, etc., so you'll always be ready to collect. Take samples of waters that have meaning to you: for instance, water from wells or springs, samples of rivers and oceans visited, rainwater that falls during powerful storms, or melt from the first snow. I collected a piece of ice from a glacier during a trip to Iceland!

To charge your waters, let the jars sit out under the desired conditions (direct sunlight, full moonlight, lightning storm, etc.), particularly on significant dates or during specific astronomical alignments.

Bottle each water and label carefully (because they all look alike). Use them to add strength to your spells and potions.

Susan Pesznecker

August 9
Sunday

3rd ♈

☽ v/c 3:50 pm

☽ → ♉ 9:28 pm

Color of the Day: Orange
Incense of the Day: Marigold

A Serenity Spell

In the country, where you can truly experience the season, a sweet serenity settles over the land now. The harvest is underway, and nature begins to relax. This is also a good time for you to experience a little serenity.

Perform this spell outside in the evening. If that's not possible, perform it at your altar. You'll need a calming herb, such as lavender, fresh or dried. Sit on the ground or floor. Inhale the herb's scent and say:

*Earth spirit, serenity has
settled over you.*

*Earth spirit, share your calming
energy with me too.*

Feel the earth's energy flow into you. Feel it enter your spine, your arms, your neck, etc. Do shoulder rolls. Allow your neck to go limp. Stay in this state for as long as it's comfortable.

Return to your normal state. Leave the herb as an offering. You should now feel a sense of peace and calm.

James Kambos

August 10
Monday

3rd ♉

Color of the Day: Silver
Incense of the Day: Lily

Technology Protection Spell

With the sun and Mercury both in Leo now, it's an excellent time to do magic that protects items of technology from mishaps such as viruses, theft, and damage. Cast this spell on your cell phone, tablet, and/or computer to harness the power of Leo to do just that.

You will need a piece of technology to enchant and four white candles in holders. Make a square with the candles, place the item of technology inside the square, then light the candles. Envision the astrological glyph for Leo (♌) hovering above the technology and then slowly descending until it is finally absorbed by the item. As this happens, say:

*In Leo, both now stand, the sun
and Mercury, hand in hand.*

*Aligned with the current astrology,
I command you to protect my technology!*

Remove the item from the candles, but let them burn out safely on their own.

Devin Hunter

August 11
Tuesday

3rd ♉
4th Quarter 12:45 pm

Color of the Day: Red
Incense of the Day: Geranium

Pop-Up Protection

A quick and delicious means for gaining a bit of magical protection is to empower some popcorn kernels with protection energy and then pop them and eat the snack. Air-popped corn is preferred, but in a pinch, microwave popcorn will do.

To empower the kernels, hold them in your hands (or hold the microwave packet) and say:

*To all who consume, your gift will be
sent, kernels of corn, protection imbue.*

*Magical energy freely lent, bursting
with power to protect and renew.*

Pop the corn and enjoy it perhaps with a light sprinkle of salt, which will also lend protective qualities.

Michael Furie

August 12
Wednesday

4th ♉

☽ v/c 3:55 am

☽ → ♊ 9:46 am

Color of the Day: Brown
Incense of the Day: Lilac

Magical honey

Honey bees are associated with industriousness, productivity, teamwork, and business. Ethically collected honey is a perfect addition to spells for career advancement, finding employment, or just getting a lot of work done.

Place your jar of honey in the sun, and see how it glows with its own golden light. Imagine the sun beaming successful, industrious energy straight into the honey, heating it up with motivation and inspiration. With this strong, vibrant feeling in mind, use a permanent marker to write the words *It is done!* on the jar. You may choose different words to suit your specific situation, but this phrase covers the general sense of accomplishing work-related goals.

Set aside the jar of honey for days when you need an extra push to be productive at work, before a job interview, or when you are overwhelmed. Add it to your morning coffee, cereal, toast, or tea to fortify you for the day.

Kate Freuler

 August 13
Thursday

4th ♊

Color of the Day: Green
Incense of the Day: Carnation

Tie Up a Ribbon

The Festival of Diana began on this day in Rome. She was the goddess of the moon, animals, and the hunt. During this time, festival-goers would write their petitions and wishes on ribbons and tie them to trees. You can connect to those ancient energies and with Diana on this day.

Take your own piece of ribbon and write your petition or wish on it. Hold the ribbon in your hands and say:

Diana ,goddess of the moon, take my petition and give me a boon.

Now clear your mind and take a deep breath. While exhaling, feel your energy connecting to the ribbon. Tie the ribbon to a branch of a tree that you will pass by often, placing your intention into the universe.

Charlynn Walls

August 14
Friday

4th ♊

☽ v/c 7:19 am

☽ → ♋ 7:35 pm

Color of the Day: Coral
Incense of the Day: Rose

A Crystal Energy Drink

No, this isn't your morning smoothie! This is a gem elixir to help you get the most out of your day. You'll need a small, clear drinking glass and a larger one; you're going to put one inside the other. You'll also need a gemstone. Select from the following list, or (if you're experienced) use a stone you already work with.

- *Carnelian:* Energy and vitality

- *Citrine:* New beginnings

- *Rose quartz:* Universal love

- *Sodalite:* Cleansing and purification

- *Amethyst:* Peace and spirituality

- *Tektite:* Grounding and discipline

Place the stone in the smaller glass. Place the smaller glass in the larger one, and put some purified drinking water around it, but not too much—you don't want the glass to float away!

Let this bathe in the sunlight for a day, then remove the smaller glass and drink the energy of the crystal and the life force of the sun.

Charlie Rainbow Wolf

August 15
Saturday

4th ♋

Color of the Day: Indigo
Incense of the Day: Magnolia

Planting Dimes for the Fae

Legend has it that faeries and other wee folk have a penchant for shiny things—especially dimes! Depending on the country in which you live, gather dimes or the smallest silver coins offered in your local currency. Shine up thirteen of these dimes (or other coins) with soap and water. Put these in your right-hand pocket and carry a small packet of honey with you to your favorite natural spot where you expect the wee folk to have a presence—ideally in your own garden, backyard, or neighborhood!

Legend also has it that we should offer gratitude to the fae in order to gain their protection or—at the very least—keep them from tricking us too severely. "Plant" the dimes in the earth by simply pushing them into the soil, and say this prayer:

*Faeries true and faeries bright, I
thank you now with love and light.*

Drip some honey on each planting, knowing that you are spreading a little astral light to inhabitants of a realm that can always benefit from a bit more respectful acknowledgment.

Raven Digitalis

August 16
Sunday

4th ♋

☽ v/c 7:59 pm

Color of the Day: Amber
Incense of the Day: Juniper

Dragon Protection Spell

Late summer is a good time to do a protection spell or to renew previous protection spells. This simple spell can be layered over existing wards to reinforce them.

Gather these supplies:

• A black candle in a holder

• A small statue or picture of a dragon

Sit where you won't be disturbed for thirty minutes. Light the candle, saying:

I ignite the dragon's protection
for my home, inside and out.

Hold the statue or picture of the dragon. Close your eyes. Imagine protective energy originating in your ritual space and expanding outward, filling a sphere encompassing your home and grounds, above and below. Now imagine your dragon perched on top of the sphere, protecting it. Focus and hold the image as long as possible, then let it go.

Place the statue or picture in a prominent place in your home. This is where the protective energy is stored. You can tap into additional protective energy when necessary by looking or touching the dragon, or (if away from home) closing your eyes and visualizing the dragon extending protective energy to you wherever you are.

Cerridwen Iris Shea

August 17
Monday

4th ♋
☽ → ♌ 1:38 am

Color of the Day: Lavender
Incense of the Day: Neroli

Morning Commute Charm

D raw or buy a small picture of a
five-pointed star (pentagram)
and place it on an easily accessible
part of your car's dashboard, with the
single point facing upward. After it's
in place, trace your finger along the
star and visualize yourself driving free
of distractions, accidents, and heavy
traffic.

When you encounter horrible
traffic, dangerous weather conditions,
road construction, or delays, touch the
pentacle and say:

Safe and quick this trip shall be,

Clear and pleasant roads I see!

The charm will activate when you
speak the couplet, and your driving
condition will improve momentarily.
Using this charm can also help you
increase your patience, concentration,
and attentiveness while driving.

Ari & Jason Mankey

NOTES:

August 18
Tuesday

4th ♌

New Moon 10:42 pm

Color of the Day: Gray
Incense of the Day: Cedar

Get Your Mojo Back Spell

Sometimes life and love can really shake our confidence. We know we're awesome. If only the people around us would figure that out!

For this spell, take a dark blue candle and use a small blade or wooden pick to inscribe it with symbols and words describing all the things you like about yourself. Enhance these markings with silver ink to make these qualities shine! Then take small pieces of paper and write "labels" of all the things specific people—or our culture in general—have said about you that you know aren't true. Place these labels all around the candle on your altar.

Finally, place a fire-proof dish on your altar and focus deeply on your strengths. Light the candle. Take each label in turn and read it aloud and laugh at the absurdity of it. With passion, state:

I reject this label!

Then carefully touch the label to the candle's flame. Set it in the fireproof dish and watch it burn, knowing that this untruth no longer applies to you. Repeat with all the other labels, and then, as the candle burns down, focus on how wonderful you know yourself to be.

Thuri Calafia

August 19
Wednesday

1st ♌

☽ v/c 1:38 am

☽ → ♍ 4:20 am

Color of the Day: White
Incense of the Day: Honeysuckle

A Walk in the Sun

Take a summer walk today. But remember to protect yourself; don't walk when the summer sun is high. (One of the sun's least welcome gifts is melanoma.) Go out close to dawn or dusk for your walk. Can you discern any changes in the light? How is the sunlight today different from what it was in February or May? One of the gifts of light is shadow. As you walk, look at the shadows around you. What do they reveal? Look at the shadow you cast. Do you cast a long shadow, either literally or metaphorically?

As you walk, greet the people you meet with a cheerful smile. Whisper blessings to the trees and plants. Notice that plants that seemed strong in June may be dry in August. Is there a lesson for us humans in the fact that some of Gaia's green children thrive in full sun while others prefer the shade?

Barbara Ardinger

August 20
Thursday

1st ♍

☽ v/c 11:37 pm

Color of the Day: Crimson
Incense of the Day: Myrrh

Islamic New Year (begins at
sundown on Aug. 19)

Money Meditation
Mini-Boot Camp

Choose a seven-day period to perform the following meditation each morning, holding your wallet or purse in your hands or lap while you meditate. Begin with this:

The flow of money in my life is increasing in a way that is correct and good for me. Higher self, what can I do today to support this healthy flow of money?

Sit in meditation for a few minutes or as long as you'd like, remaining open to guidance. Remember, you don't need an elaborate plan; you're simply looking for your next action step. Write it down and carry out your higher self's guidance throughout the day. Repeat this process each morning for a week.

This practice is a powerful commitment to co-creating prosperity, and it may challenge you to step beyond your comfort zone as you break out of the ego's narrow perceptions of what is possible and embrace the ever-expanding reality of your higher self.

Melissa Tipton

August 21
Friday

1st ♏

☽ → ♎ 5:16 am

Color of the Day: Pink
Incense of the Day: Mint

Safe Travels!

For this spell, you'll need the following items:

- 2 candles (and holders)
- A bowl
- A small object
- 2 pinches of dirt from outside your home
- Salt
- Water
- A feather
- A clover

Place the candles on your altar, several inches apart. Put the bowl between them, and place the small object in the bowl.

Light one candle and say:

This is my home.

Light the other candle and say:

This is my destination.

Sprinkle the object with a pinch of dirt and say:

My home is my sanctuary.

Sprinkle the object with salt and say:

May I be protected as I travel over earth.

Sprinkle the object with water and say:

May I be protected as I travel over water.

Pass the feather over the object and say:

May I be protected as I travel through the air.

Place the clover on the object and say:

May I find luck throughout my travels.

Sprinkle another pinch of dirt on the object and say:

May I return safely home.

Extinguish the candles and carry the object with you on your travels.

Susan Pesznecker

August 22
Saturday

1st ♎

☉ → ♍ 11:45 am

Color of the Day: Brown
Incense of the Day: Sandalwood

harvest Thanks

In many places, gardens are in full production mode at this time of year. If you're growing your own garden, don't forget to give back to the land spirits as you enjoy the fruits of the earth (and your own labor). Whether your harvest is bountiful or slim, you should remember and acknowledge those spirits.

Gather together a selection of your harvest, be it food or herbs, and make a small biodegradable (all-natural) bundle. At the edge of your garden or land, place it carefully, saying:

> *To the spirits of land, I offer my gratitude for this harvest. May it please and nourish you, as it has nourished me. I honor our connection.*

Laura Tempest Zakroff

August 23
Sunday

1st ♎

☽ v/c 12:20 am

☽ → ♏ 6:16 am

Color of the Day: Yellow
Incense of the Day: Frankincense

Back to School Spell

School has started or will soon. This spell will help you focus on clarity, balance, and wisdom. It will help you achieve your academic goals.

You'll need an amethyst gem or crystal or a smooth amethyst stone. These are available at gem shops and are inexpensive. Amethyst helps you attract wisdom and achieve clarity. You'll also need a violet-colored candle (for balance) in a holder and a piece of paper. Light the candle. Then write your academic goal on the paper. Wrap the paper around the amethyst. Ground and center. Holding the paper and stone, say:

> *My goal in school I will achieve.*
>
> *Amethyst, give me the clarity and wisdom to succeed.*

Hide the paper and amethyst and extinguish the candle. When you notice the spell is working, discard the paper. Keep the amethyst and candle for other spells. Perform this same spell separately for each of your academic goals.

James Kambos

August 24
Monday

1st ♏︎

Color of the Day: Ivory
Incense of the Day: Hyssop

To Gain Control of a Situation

Life gets chaotic sometimes, but we don't have to surrender to the chaos. In fact, sometimes to do so would be disastrous. Today, with the moon in Scorpio, we can use the astrological influences available to seize control in these moments.

To cast this spell, you will need a blue candle in a holder. Light the candle and gaze into the flame. Focus on your breathing and the moment of stillness and silence at the end of each breath. Visualize the light from the candle expanding to reach every aspect of your life, leaving nothing untouched. Say:

Light of Scorpio, hear my claim.
I take control with this flame!

Chaos and confusion no longer to reign, control is mine to obtain!

When you feel a sense of peace wash over you, your job is done. Blow out the candle and repeat as necessary.

Devin Hunter

August 25
Tuesday

1st ♏︎
☽ v/c 2:27 am
☽ → ♐ 8:49 am
2nd Quarter 1:58 pm

Color of the Day: Scarlet
Incense of the Day: Ylang-ylang

Harvest Something from Nature

From Lughnasadh at the beginning of the month, we have reached harvest time. Not all of us have gardens or seasonal crops that are dependent upon our ability to harvest the food they create. However, we can usually find something to harvest in a spot out in nature, even if only a public park.

Go to an area with plants and grass and find something to harvest. It could be something as simple as a clover and should not be anything that would be illegal to take. Whatever you are able to harvest, take it home and let it dry, perhaps pressing it in a book. Keep it for the rest of the year as a symbol of the great cycle of growth and decline and as a charm against famine.

Michael Furie

August 26
Wednesday

2nd ♐

Color of the Day: Topaz
Incense of the Day: Bay laurel

Goldenrod Bouquet

Goldenrod is a common weed that is easily found along roadsides and in fields in late summer. Its bright golden top makes it perfect for money and luck spells, and it looks pretty too.

Gather a bundle of goldenrod, anywhere from five to ten stalks. Get a vase of an appropriate size and fill it with water. Find a sunny spot to sit in, and lay the goldenrod pieces in front of you.

Pick up one stalk of goldenrod and hold it in the sunlight. The sun is like a golden coin beaming prosperous energy down onto the stalk. State something you wish to obtain, then place the plant in the vase.

Keep your intentions specific and simple, such as "money for dance lessons" or "new school clothes." Repeat this process for all your stalks of goldenrod, then place the bouquet near your front door. Once the flowers wither, dispose of them outside, sending your wishes into the universe.

Kate Freuler

August 27
Thursday

2nd ♐

☽ v/c 8:00 am

☽ → ♑ 1:37 pm

Color of the Day: Turquoise
Incense of the Day: Balsam

Create Abundance

At this time of year, we see some of the first harvests coming in, including grains that were planted early in the spring. You can take some of that wheat and bake it into bread. There are many good recipes for quick breads that can be made by hand or with a bread machine. As you are baking the bread, think about bringing the blessings of abundance into your life. Vocalize the following:

As this bread rises throughout the day, abundance shall come my way.

Share the bread with family and friends and spare a little as an offering to Thor on this Thursday. This will increase the spell's impact, as it is a sympathetic gesture of creating abundance for others.

Charlynn Walls

August 28
Friday

2nd ♑

Color of the Day: Rose
Incense of the Day: Alder

A Commitment Spell

You don't have to commit to another person to work this spell, although if you're in a relationship and want to take it to the next level, it will strengthen your bond. This is a spell to work when you want to pledge yourself to a person, a project, or even just some new-school-year self-discipline. You'll need a white candle in a holder, something to light it with, and a cabbage leaf.

As you light the candle, say:

By candlelight my work begins,

I'll see it through until the end.

And by my soul I will not quit,

I'll work hard and make the best of it.

Pinch out the candle and wrap it in the cabbage leaf. Repeat this spell nightly until the cabbage leaf becomes too decayed to use, then put the leaf outside to disintegrate or blow away or whatever the leaf wants to do. It doesn't matter where you put it as long as it's out in the elements (as opposed to throwing it away). Keep the candle safe until you need it for your next commitment spell.

Charlie Rainbow Wolf

NOTES:

August 29
Saturday

2nd ♑

☽ v/c 3:31 pm

☽ → ♒ 8:37 pm

Color of the Day: Black
Incense of the Day: Pine

Alchemical Mercury, Sulfur, and Salt

Western hermetic alchemical science has long acknowledged the elements of mercury, sulfur, and salt as the building blocks of life. Whether viewed physically or energetically, these elements are said to uphold all physical reality in varying degrees and combinations.

Light a black candle, a red candle, and a white candle in holders in front of you at dusk. Place the black one on your left, red in the middle, and white on your right.

On a small piece of paper, use red marker to write, *I alchemize _____ into _____*, or one perceived negative into a perceived positive. For example, *I alchemize fear into acceptance* or *I alchemize fatigue into alertness*. Feel free to write as many affirmations as you wish.

Having cast your circle or called the powers that be, carefully burn the paper with a lick of each candle's flame. Place its ashes on top of a small piece of tinfoil (representing mercury), and top it with a match (sulfur) and a sprinkle of salt. Crumple this all together. Declare your intentions and store the spell in a special secret place.

Raven Digitalis

August 30
Sunday

2nd ≈

Color of the Day: Gold
Incense of the Day: Eucalyptus

A Wish Bracelet Spell

Just for fun and whimsy, it's great to make wish bracelets. But lest you think they can't be powerful, think again! Magic is all about what you put into it; both clarity of intention and follow-through count.

For this spell, all you'll need is some cotton embroidery thread in the three colors that best represent your wish. As you braid the threads together, visualize your wish as already manifested. Once the braid is finished, tie a knot at one-quarter the length, visualizing the first thing you will do to achieve your wish. Tie another knot at the halfway point, visualizing the second thing you will do. Repeat with a third knot at three-quarters the length, then tie the bracelet on your wrist (or ankle) with three more knots. Say:

By all the power of three times three,
my wish now manifests. So mote it be!

By the time the bracelet wears off naturally, your wish should be true.

Thuri Calafia

August 31
Monday

2nd ≈

Color of the Day: Silver
Incense of the Day: Clary sage

National Trail Mix Day

It's National Trail Mix Day! Mix up some delicious magic today by choosing trail mix ingredients according to your intentions, and empowering each one before you add it to the mix.

Of course, you'll need some nuts and/or seeds: choose almonds for beauty, walnuts for intelligence, hazelnuts for wisdom, pistachios for breaking old patterns, pecans for employment, cashews for prosperity, pumpkin seeds for harmony, and sunflower seeds for strength. Next, add some dried fruit: consider raisins for fertility, cherries for attraction, blueberries for protection, cranberries for clarity, and pineapple for luck. You might also add chocolate chips for romance or colorful chocolate candy for joy. (Please don't feel limited by these suggestions! If there's another magical ingredient you'd like to add, go for it.)

Blend it all together, and take a final moment to empower the mix with your overall intention. Eat it alone or share it with friends.

Tess Whitehurst

September

The equinox happens toward the end of this month, heralding the beginning of autumn in the Northern Hemisphere and the start of spring in the Southern Hemisphere. An equinox happens when the sun crosses the celestial equator, an imaginary line in the sky not unlike our Earth's own equator. It's on the equinox that the sun rises due east and sets due west. This is why people often go to famous landmarks to watch the rising or setting of the sun on the equinoxes and solstices. In our ever-changing world, it's nice to know there are at least some constants!

Astrologically, the autumnal equinox is when the sun sign of Libra begins. It's fitting, as this is the time when day and night are of equal length, and Libra is the sign of the scales. The full moon that corresponds with this event is called the Harvest Moon or the Corn Moon. The few days around the equinox and the full moon bring a period in which everything is ripening and full of energy. It all seems to be coming into fullness, preparing either for the coming of winter or the start of the growing season.

Charlie Rainbow Wolf

September 1
Tuesday

2nd ♒

☽ v/c 12:56 am

☽ → ♓ 5:34 am

Color of the Day: Black
Incense of the Day: Ginger

An Aster Love Spell

In September, asters reach their peak. They are an old favorite to use in love spells. For this spell, you'll need the petals from one purple aster. You can find asters easily at a florist. You'll also need a red candle in a holder, a square piece of burgundy fabric, and a red ribbon.

Place the petals on the fabric and tie up the corners with the ribbon. Light the candle and hold the bundle as you speak these words of power:

This candle I light of brightest red,

Bring me one who'll woo my heart and turn my head.

Aster, flower of love, I wrap in cloth the color of wine,

Bring me the one who'll be mine.

Let the candle burn down for a while, and hide the bundle.

After the spell works, scatter the petals upon the earth. Keep the candle and fabric as keepsakes, but don't use them for magic again.

James Kambos

September 2
Wednesday

2nd ♓

🌕 Full Moon 1:22 am

Color of the Day: Yellow
Incense of the Day: Lilac

An Apple Spell

In many areas this is the time for harvesting autumn foods. Apples frequently appear in folklore, and for many reasons. In this spell, we're going to use an apple to welcome deities into your life. You'll need an apple, a knife, a bowl of water, a tablespoon of lemon juice, and a nail or hook.

Peel the apple, trying to keep the peel in one long strip. When the apple is peeled, plunge it in a bowl of water to which you've added the lemon juice. Set the peel to one side. Quarter the apple and take out the seeds.

Eat the apple, then place the seeds outside the main door of your home, alongside the path or next to the step. Hang the peel up over your door. Let your thoughts reinforce this spell by believing that you're safe, secure, and held in the arms of the Goddess.

Charlie Rainbow Wolf

September 3
Thursday

3rd ♓

☽ v/c 10:34 am

☽ → ♈ 4:22 pm

Color of the Day: Purple
Incense of the Day: Clove

Path Cleaning

The Akwambo festival, which is celebrated in Ghana in early September, is an occasion when paths to streams, shrines, and holy places are swept. I think it's disrespectful when New Agers and Neopagans read about a ritual that sounds interesting and just pick it up and celebrate it however they want. Doing this is taking a ritual—and a belief system—entirely out of its proper context. But we're all guilty of this, aren't we?

While the idea of path cleaning and giving thanks to our ancestors is a good one, let's not engage in cultural piracy. We can do our own kind of path cleaning! Give thanks to your ancestors (and neighbors) that you have a path, both literal and metaphorical, to walk. When you walk, carry a trash bag and pick up some trash. At home, neaten up your sidewalk or front yard as you give thanks to Hygeia and Hestia.

Barbara Ardinger

September 4
Friday

3rd ♈

Color of the Day: White
Incense of the Day: Yarrow

Back to School Charm

Making new friends can be tough, especially for young kids just starting school. Here is a charm I made for my daughter on her first day to attract friendships and fun in an unfamiliar classroom.

Gather these materials:

- Colorful beads shaped like hearts or other friendship symbols
- Thin cord for stringing

Hold all the beads in your hands and visualize your child surrounded by other children, laughing and playing. Imagine your child having a great time at school and feeling happiness as they connect with other kids. See the beads glowing with a pink aura.

String the beads on the cord, continuing to visualize, until it is about five inches long. Tie the ends together, creating a circle of good vibes. Tie this securely to the zipper on your child's school bag.

Should the string get broken accidentally, not to worry—it will release friendly energy!

Kate Freuler

September 5
Saturday

3rd ♈

Color of the Day: Brown
Incense of the Day: Sage

Witch's Bath for Renewal

There is a lot of earth energy in the world today, but not quite the grounded type of earth energy that we are used to. Today is more about the transformational and regenerative properties of earth. Cast this spell to harness the energy of renewal.

To a warm bath, add the following:

• 2 cups sea salt

• 13 drops each of lavender, patchouli, and grapefruit essential oils

• ½ cup dried milk

Swirl the ingredients together in a clockwise motion using your hand, and say:

Powers of the earth that rise,
bless this water and make it wise.

Bring renewal and clarity,
bring strength and sincerity.

With these words, I make it so,
by these elements, the spell will flow!

If you don't have a bathtub, mix the ingredients in a white bowl with warm water, then pour that over yourself in the shower. Be sure to avoid getting any in your eyes.

Devin Hunter

September 6
Sunday

3rd ♈

☽ v/c 12:45 am

☽ → ♉ 4:43 am

Color of the Day: Amber
Incense of the Day: Hyacinth

Abbots Bromley Horn Dance

Today in the English town of Abbots Bromley, folk dancers will hold thousand-year-old reindeer horns and dance the oldest-known dance in Britain: the Abbots Bromley Horn Dance. While no one knows exactly how old the dance really is, carbon dating from one of the horns suggests it's been practiced every year since 1050 CE. Locals believe the dance was performed (traditionally by men) to bless the land and promote abundant crops.

Take a cue from this unbroken pagan custom and dance your own blessing dance today. Put on some music that helps you feel connected to your pagan ancestors (we all have them!) and the earth. Light some earthy incense or diffuse an earthy fragrance. If you have horns available (real or costume), wear them or hold them near your head. Then dance the perimeter of your space, inside or out, as you consciously honor your own wildness and the aliveness of the earth.

Tess Whitehurst

September 7
Monday

3rd ♉

Color of the Day: White
Incense of the Day: Narcissus

Labor Day (US) –
Labour Day (Canada)

Magickal Workings

Today in the United States, we recognize the labor movement and the contributions and achievements of American workers. It is a great time to recognize and honor the deities that you partner with on a regular basis.

Think about the deities you work with and determine what a fitting offering would be for them. Gather those items together and write a small note of thanks, then put them all in a small bowl that can stay outside overnight. The bowl can be placed on a porch, balcony, or windowsill or at the base of a tree. Simply say *thank you*. You'll be surprised at how much this simple recognition can improve your relationship with those deities.

Charlynn Walls

September 8
Tuesday

3rd ♉

☽ v/c 8:47 am

☽ → ♊ 5:28 pm

Color of the Day: Scarlet
Incense of the Day: Cinnamon

Back to School Success Spell

Back-to-school energy is in the air, making it a wonderful time to embark on a new course of study. If there's a topic you feel drawn to explore or an area in which you'd like to hone your skills, be it magical or mundane, use this incantation to marshal support for your studies. Fill in the blank with your topic of choice (for example, tarot, baking, etc).

*I call upon the spirit of
(fill in the blank)!*

As I embark upon this path of study, new learning, and growth, ignite my curiosity; help my thoughts and actions flow.

May all I learn expand my view and hone my talents true.

Optional: Make a vial of carrier oil, like almond or jojoba, with a few drops each of rosemary and lemon essential oils, which aid in concentration. Hold the vial as you say the incantation, charging it with your intention. Dab the oil on pulse points before studying.

Melissa Tipton

September 9
Wednesday

3rd ♊

Color of the Day: Topaz
Incense of the Day: Marjoram

The Free Exercise of Will

There are times when we may feel blocked or stifled or shy and unable to fully express ourselves. The element of fire is linked to willpower and strength, so it helps to reconnect to this element in order to rekindle our inner fire and confidence.

For this spell, you will need a red candle and a hand mirror. Light the candle safely and gaze into the flame. Remember that as warm-blooded creatures, we all have a genuine direct inner connection to the element of fire. Look into the mirror and feel your confidence, drive, and willpower flare up, and say:

Strength and passion, personal power; inner fire emerge this hour.

Return to me my confident will, that my true self be fulfilled.

Extinguish the candle. Repeat the ritual as often as needed.

Michael Furie

September 10
Thursday

3rd ♊
4th Quarter 5:26 am 2

Color of the Day: Green
Incense of the Day: Jasmine

Sweet Love Spell For the Sweetest Day

What do you have to offer to love? Make a list, however long you like, of all the blessings and gifts that go with having a romance with you. Next, list the qualities you seek in a partner. Be honest with yourself, but remember that if all you seek are superficial qualities, you will draw a superficial relationship.

Take a scrap of cotton cloth of a color you associate with romance, and cut it into a heart shape. Pile some dried rose petals, lavender, cinnamon chips, and barley in the center of the heart. Then concentrate on all the things on both lists while fluffing the herbs and chanting:

I know what I bring to the party,

And I choose love, so love chooses me.

I accept and deserve the best of the best,

By the gods, so mote it be!

Repeat the chant thirteen times, then tie up the charm with a bright ribbon and keep it on your person whenever you go out.

Thuri Calafia

September 11
Friday

4th ♊
☽ v/c 12:48 am
☽ → ♋ 4:23 am

Color of the Day: Purple
Incense of the Day: Rose

Lost Loved One Remembrance Spell

Many Witches associate Samhain/Halloween with ancestors and lost loved ones, but such rites can be practiced at any time of year. Most years on September 11, I think a great deal about my family and those I've lost over the years. Reaching out to loved ones who have moved beyond the veil is not complicated and can be done whenever you need their guidance or presence.

Place a picture of your deceased loved one on your altar (or write their name on a piece of paper), and place something they loved in this life next to it. Follow this by repeating their name several times and then saying:

I love and miss you and long for your voice.

Come to this place now if it be your choice.

So mote it be.

Feel their presence around you and speak to them as you did when they were in this world.

Ari & Jason Mankey

September 12
Saturday

4th ♋

Color of the Day: Gray
Incense of the Day: Patchouli

Autumnal Altar Reset

Spring cleaning was great six months ago, but now it's time to get our house in order for the colder tides of autumn and winter.

Approach the altar(s) or shrine(s) in your home. Meditate on the physical items on each, considering how each one serves as a focal point or catalyst for your magickal work, ancestor worship, or other esoteric work.

One by one, remove each object from the altar or shrine and reset the space. Cleanse each item, tablecloth, and nearby sacred object with incense (a natural resin if possible) and wash it with soap and water (if appropriate). You may consider going throughout your home and doing the same with other sacred pieces.

As you reset the altar or shrine, use your intuition to put some of the items back in the same place and others in a different place. You may find that some objects "want" to leave the altar and others "want" to be honored in their place. Once it feels complete, declare:

Autumnal tides and powers
that be, this altar is enchanted
by fire, earth, air, and sea!

Raven Digitalis

September 13
Sunday

4th ♋

☽ v/c 8:05 am
☽ → ♌ 11:32 am

Color of the Day: Yellow
Incense of the Day: Marigold

Finding Balance

Do you spend more time on daily chores than on your spiritual life? Do you feel a need for less work and more family? You need a balancing spell.

Gather these items:

- 2 three-foot-long ribbons (½ to 1-inch wide), one black and one white
- Paper and pen

Reflect on those parts of your life that feel out of balance. Write down eight that seem to take up too much time and eight that aren't taking up enough, or perhaps eight qualities or behaviors you'd like to do more or less of. Write the "positives" on one colored ribbon and the "negatives" on the other ribbon.

Tie the two ribbons together with a square knot (a balanced knot) and then repeat until you have tied a total of eight knots. For each knot, say:

Black and white and dark and light,

I search for balance, day and night.

Bring an ordered life to me,

That I may feel more harmony.

Carry the knotted cords with you as a reminder until your goals are reached.

Susan Pesznecker

September 14
Monday

4th ♌

Color of the Day: Ivory
Incense of the Day: Lily

Creative Energy Spell

Autumn often involves juggling many different parts of life. But creative energy is important to overall vitality, and this spell will help restore your creative energy.

You will need these supplies:

- A yellow candle in a holder
- 3 tarot cards: the Nine of Cups, the Sun, the Ace of Pentacles
- Your favorite music
- A favorite craft (writing, knitting, drawing, baking, etc.)

Place the tarot cards in front of the candle. Light the candle, saying:

I light my creative flame.

Turn on the music, and spend one hour of uninterrupted time engaged in your favorite craft. You'll feel revitalized! Be sure to extinguish the candle.

Cerridwen Iris Shea

September 15
Tuesday

4th ♌

☽ v/c 11:09 am

☽ → ♍ 2:37 pm

Color of the Day: Red
Incense of the Day: Basil

A Letter to the Deceased

The apple harvest has begun, and in occult belief apples are associated with the dead. In this spell, an apple is used as an offering to the deceased.

Drape your altar with black fabric. On it, place a black candle in a holder, white paper, a black ink pen, and an apple. Think of the deceased, then silently begin writing a letter like this:

*Sweet spirit, now that you
are in death's embrace,*

*I ache because I can no
longer see your face.*

*The words I write are for
you and you alone,*

*They're sent with love, as if you
were still flesh and bone.*

Continue writing and say whatever else you wish to say. Show no one the letter. Snuff out the candle. Wrap the letter around the apple and bury it. Your letter has been received. Don't be surprised if the deceased contacts you in a dream.

James Kambos

September 16
Wednesday

4th ♍

Color of the Day: White
Incense of the Day: Honeysuckle

Strong Foundation Spell

At number 16 in the Major Arcana of the Tarot, we find the Tower card. This can be a scary card to pull, as it often signifies that something is about to fall apart. But the Tower also reminds us to check our foundations—are we moving too fast for our own good?

Keep an eye out for a small rock or stone that catches your attention. If you get a good feeling while holding it, take the rock home and clean it. With a permanent marker, draw a star and a square on opposite sides of the rock. The star represents upward motion, and the square symbolizes foundation.

Keep the rock with you, and when you're wondering if you're making the right choice, roll the rock in your hands and then open them. If the star is facing up, focus on the next step. If the square is facing up, take more time before you move forward.

Laura Tempest Zakroff

☾ September 17
Thursday

4th ♍

New Moon 7:00 am

☽ v/c 7:42 am

☽ → ♎ 2:56 pm

Color of the Day: Turquoise
Incense of the Day: Clove

New Moon, New Beginning

When the moon is new, we're sitting in the dark. What can we do in the dark? Remember that darkness is good. Babies grow in the darkness of the womb. Seeds germinate in the darkness under the ground. A new moon is a golden opportunity to begin something.

Cast your circle in the dark and consider what you need to begin again. A term paper? A work project? Place the Queen of Pentacles from the Tarot on your altar and light at least one white candle in a holder. Gather some moonstones and name each one for something that needs to begin again. Keep them on your altar all month. Say:

*Blessed new moon, gracious queen,
teach me what to plant and grow.*

*I am rooted in the darkness. Help
me grow with you toward the light,*

*Into fruition, into
understanding, into success.*

So mote it be!

Barbara Ardinger

♡ September 18
Friday

1st ♎

Color of the Day: Rose
Incense of the Day: Vanilla

An Offering to Venus

Friday is sacred to Venus, the Roman goddess of love, beauty, and seduction. Today, set aside a small space dedicated to this goddess of love, welcoming her powers into your life. Some items that symbolize Venus are seashells, rose quartz, mirrors, and sweet-smelling flowers.

Gather these together in an esthetically pleasing way, and place a piece of chocolate in the center. Light a red candle in a holder on your shrine, and envision the type of love and beauty you'd like to manifest in your life.

Break the piece of chocolate in half. Leave half on your mini-altar as an offering to Venus. Eat the other half and know that you are attracting love and beauty into your life. Repeat every Friday until you feel it is done or you manifest what you desire. Be sure to extinguish the candle.

Kate Freuler

September 19
Saturday

1st ♎

☽ v/c 10:29 am

☽ → ♏ 2:33 pm

Color of the Day: Blue
Incense of the Day: Ivy

Rosh hashanah (begins at sundown on Sept. 18)

Rosh hashanah

L'Shanah Tova! It's Rosh Hashanah, the Jewish New Year. Traditionally, it's a time to forgive and be forgiven, to release old challenges and mistakes, and to bless the fresh new cycle ahead. A particularly magical Rosh Hashanah custom involves dipping apple slices in honey to fill the year with sweetness. The apple relates to health, as well as the feminine aspect of God, known as the Shekhinah. The honey symbolizes the sweet blessings we hope the Shekhinah will shower upon us.

To create your own version of this ritual, slice an apple. Say a gratitude blessing over the apple in a way that feels powerful for you. Dip a slice in honey and take a bite. Then speak to God/dess from your heart, respectfully requesting an incredibly sweet, healthy, and joyful new cycle. You can do this alone or share the ritual with a partner or group.

Tess Whitehurst

September 20
Sunday

1st ♏

Color of the Day: Orange
Incense of the Day: Almond

An Apple Spell for Finding Love

Since it is apple season and these special fruits are known to be otherworldly reservoirs of magical power, they can offer us assistance in important work such as healing or finding love. An apple, when cut through the middle, usually holds a natural pentacle of five points to hold its seeds. This is perhaps one of the reasons that the fruit is linked to witchcraft. In any event, a quick, effective spell to draw love requires only a single apple.

Hold an apple with both hands and think of being in love. Mentally and emotionally conjure up feelings of joyful romance. Take a bite of the apple and keep building this vision. With each bite of apple, intensify the feeling. By eating the apple, you're taking in the magic and responsibility of the spell. When finished, bury the core in the earth to release the magic.

Michael Furie

September 21
Monday

1st ♏

☽ v/c 2:13 pm

☽ → ♐ 3:32 pm

Color of the Day: Silver
Incense of the Day: Rosemary

UN International Day of Peace

A Chant for Peace

Today is the UN International Day of Peace, and the approaching Jupiter-Pluto conjunction makes this a fantastic time for bringing about positive change.

Chanting may be familiar to you, and you may have even used this phrase previously: *Nam myoho renge kyo.* This is a simple expression with transformational power. *Nam* means dedication, *myo* means wonderful, and *ho* is the law. *Renge* refers to the lotus, which grows beautiful in the mud, while *kyo* means sutra, or teaching.

Repeat these words throughout the day as a reminder to be at peace with yourself and your life and to bring that peace into the world as a whole. The phrase isn't magical; it doesn't have mystical powers. The power is within you. Chanting these words awakens the divinity in you and empowers you to be the best version of yourself that you can be. It is simple yet profound.

Charlie Rainbow Wolf

September 22
Tuesday

1st ♐

☉ → ♎ 9:31 am

Color of the Day: Maroon
Incense of the Day: Cedar

Mabon – Fall Equinox

Mabon Apple Magic

The autumn equinox is a powerful time to cultivate balance, and as it is the second harvest before the fallow period of winter, it is an especially potent time to balance what we take in or harvest versus what we release. Slice an apple in half (not through the stem end) to reveal the five-pointed star inside, a powerful symbol of balance among the elements. Choose one half to represent what you wish to harvest; the other half will represent what you wish to release.

Hold the releasing half of the apple in your hands and bring to mind the situations, thoughts, etc., that no longer serve you. Send them into the apple, then compost or bury it, giving thanks for this process of release. Hold the other half while you bring to mind all that you wish to welcome into your life, sending it into the apple. Then eat the apple, giving thanks for this bountiful harvest.

Melissa Tipton

September 23
Wednesday

1st ♐

☽ v/c 1:31 pm

☽ → ♑ 7:16 pm

2nd Quarter 9:55 pm

Color of the Day: Yellow
Incense of the Day: Lavender

The Wise Owl

Even though we'd like to think we know it all, we all could use a little more wisdom to guide us on our journey through life. On this Wednesday, work with the power of air and Athena to increase your wisdom.

Athena's totem is the owl, which represents wisdom. Find a way to incorporate the owl into your life. Change your phone's wallpaper to an owl, or wear an owl piece of jewelry today.

When you put this on your phone or person, say:

*Athena's owl sees, and provides
wisdom with ease.*

Continue through your day and let wisdom come your way!

Charlynn Walls

September 24
Thursday

2nd ♑

Color of the Day: Crimson
Incense of the Day: Mulberry

Spark Your Creativity Spell

For this spell, you'll need a pillar candle of a color you associate with creative ideas. First, use a small blade or wooden pick to carve a fire symbol (like the icon above) on the front of the candle. Then add symbols and words of the type of creative work you wish to enhance.

Hold the candle in your hands and visualize yourself creating, with joy and ease, all the things you wish to create. Allow yourself to feel the satisfaction of having your work turn out exactly as you'd hoped it would. Then visualize your work going above and beyond your wildest dreams and hopes, to critical acclaim and popularity, to worldwide approval and praise!

Let your hands flow over the symbols on the candle, filling it with your brightest hopes. Using a simple oil (such as olive or an essential oil you like), anoint the candle if you wish, and as you light it, thank your deities for giving you creative talent, and tell yourself that you are bright and talented and can accomplish anything you desire. Blessed be. (Be sure to extinguish the candle.)

Thuri Calafia

September 25
Friday

2nd ♑

☽ v/c 11:36 pm

Color of the Day: Pink
Incense of the Day: Orchid

Love and Lust Spell for Two

With your partner or lover, place the following on a small swatch of red cloth:

- A cinnamon stick (for sexual heat)

- Rose petals (for love)

- A small piece of magnetite (for attraction)

- An acorn (in honor of the god Pan)

- A small pearl (in honor of the goddess Aphrodite)

Tie the red cloth closed with a piece of red string, then seal with wax from a lit candle and anoint with ylang-ylang oil. Together with your partner, charge the magickal pouch by simultaneously holding it in your power hands and visualizing the facets of your relationship that you each want to improve.

Place the pouch between the boxspring and mattress of your bed or under a pillow so its energies can seep into your life and lovemaking. A word of caution: Pan is a great god to call upon for initiating lust, but he's also a fertility god. Plan accordingly.

Ari & Jason Mankey

September 26
Saturday

2nd ♑

☽ → ♒ 2:08 am

Color of the Day: Indigo
Incense of the Day: Sandalwood

To Summon Creativity

The moon enters the sign of Aquarius today, helping us become more social and outwardly expressive. This is an excellent time to follow your bliss and to connect to the more creative elements of your personality. Cast this spell to summon the powers of creativity from inside yourself. You will need a purple candle in a holder and something to carve it with.

Using your carving tool, etch CRTVY into the side of the candle. Light it and say:

Purple moon and Aquarius vision, creativity flows without division.

Come from within and pour yourself out; proud and strong, removing all doubt!

Let the candle burn out safely on its own.

Devin hunter

September 27
Sunday

2nd ♒

Color of the Day: Gold
Incense of the Day: Juniper

Weave a Web of Gratitude

Work this spell with three or more friends, family members, or loved ones or with your magical group. You'll need a large ball of yarn or string.

Tie one end of the ball of yarn around one person's wrist. That person begins, mentioning something they're grateful for and adding details as desired. They then pass or toss the ball to another person, ideally someone across from them. That person wraps the string (not too tightly!) around their own wrist, mentions something they're grateful for, and tosses the ball to another person. This continues until no one has anything left to mention. People might then mention goals or perhaps something they're concerned about and need support for.

When it's time to conclude, ask everyone present to marvel at the web that has been woven and how interconnected the strands are. Say together:

Each of us is but a strand, but together we raise power and strength. So mote it be!

Susan Pesznecker

September 28
Monday

2nd ♒

☽ v/c 3:18 am

☽ → ♓ 11:34 am

Color of the Day: Gray
Incense of the Day: Hyssop

Yom Kippur (begins at
sundown on Sept. 27)

Self-Forgiveness Spell

In the household I grew up in, Yom Kippur (the Day of Atonement in Judaism) meant a day and evening of phone calls where forgiveness was asked for and granted. While the practice can help us improve our relationships with other people, it can be a lot harder to forgive ourselves.

For this spell, gather these items:

• A pen

• A sheet of paper

• A lighter or match

• A cauldron

Meditate on something you've had a hard time forgiving yourself for. On the paper, write:

I forgive myself for _____.

Sign it and fold the paper into thirds. Then fold it again in thirds in the other direction until you have a folded square of nine sections.

Carefully light the paper over your cauldron and drop it inside to burn, saying three times:

Forgiveness and peace, love and release.

Once it has burned out, compost the ashes.

Laura Tempest Zakroff

September 29
Tuesday

2nd ♓

Color of the Day: Scarlet
Incense of the Day: Bayberry

Thank You For Your Work Spell

Gertrude Barnum was born on September 29, 1866. She was an organizer for the International Ladies' Garment Workers' Union and an investigator for the Department of Labor, dedicated to labor reform and safe work practices.

Today's spell is simple and powerful and a way of walking the talk. When you encounter anyone working today (at the grocery store, at school, at your workplace, etc.), simply say to them, with no explanation and no elaboration:

Thank you for all you do.

The words *thank you* matter.

Cerridwen Iris Shea

September 30
Wednesday

2nd ♓

☽ v/c 1:30 pm
☽ → ♈ 10:47 pm

Color of the Day: Brown
Incense of the Day: Bay laurel

Teatime healing

Tea is something that has been shared across cultures throughout time as a way of encouraging social bonding and supporting local economies. As a solitary teatime ritual, brew your favorite cup and sit in a dimly lit space with only yourself and the warm beverage. Warm your hands by gripping the mug. Inhale the sensual vapors steaming from the cup. Think about the different ingredients in your vessel, and take a sip to slowly taste the flavorful bouquet.

Visualize the beverage engulfed in a healing white light swirling in a deosil (clockwise) fashion. Bring to mind the areas of your life where you truly wish to invoke healing. See the beverage surrounded by the colors of the rainbow (or chakras), one by one: violet, indigo, blue, green, yellow, orange, and red. As you sip the tea, see its energy entering your chakras and your body. Finish by seeing yourself bathed in a healing white light that you will carry forth into your everyday reality.

Raven Digitalis

October

Days that turn on a breath into rapidly waning light. Wispy, high dark clouds in an orange and turquoise sky. Bright orange pumpkins carved into beautiful art and lit from inside. The eerie music of screeching cats. These fond images of October burn at a Witch's heart, calling to her even across the seasons where she's busy setting up her tent for festival. By the time October finally arrives, Witches and other magic users have already had discussions about costumes and parties, rituals and celebrations, and we look forward with happiness to the whole month of both poignantly somber and brightly playful activities.

In Celtic Europe, our ancestors acknowledged October as the last month of the summer season, with winter officially beginning on Samhain. They carved slits in squashes to keep light in the fields so they could finish their day's work, and when the custom came to America, it eventually evolved into the tradition of carving jack-o'-lanterns. American Witches often use magical symbols to carve their pumpkins, creating beacons for their Beloved Dead. In the spirit of the turn of energies at this time, we give candy to children to ensure that they, our future, will remember the sweetness inside and be good leaders when their turn comes. May we all be so blessed.

Thuri Calafia

October 1
Thursday

2nd ♈

Full Moon 5:05 pm

Color of the Day: Green
Incense of the Day: Apricot

Lucky Talisman
Full Moon Infusion

A silver coin is sometimes used to represent the full moon in divination, so why not carry it a step further and use the energy of the full moon to bless a coin to keep with you for good luck? Gather these items:

- A cauldron
- A clean quarter or silver dollar piece
- Water
- A rosemary sprig

In the light of the full moon, settle down before your cauldron and place the coin in the center of the cauldron. Fill the cauldron with water (about halfway is fine), and stir it clockwise seven times with the rosemary sprig, saying:

Luck be mine, luck come soon,
luck by light of the full moon.

Let the coin rest overnight, then pour out the water carefully. Dry the coin and carry it with you in a special place.

Laura Tempest Zakroff

October 2
Friday

3rd ♈

Color of the Day: Coral
Incense of the Day: Cypress

Bless Your Car

Magic is everywhere and can be employed for any purpose. This is a spell that can be used to help ensure that your automobile is strong, safe, and protected.

Mentally project white pentacles on each door and window of the car and also over the hood and trunk; these pentacles will help the occupants to avoid accidents, theft, or injuries while in the car. To seal the intention permanently onto the car, strongly envision the pentacles and say:

Sacred symbol, shining bright, keep me safe with your light. Magical protection, remain embedded, infused into this vehicle forever; fully secured and worry-free, as I will so mote it be!

Michael Furie

October 3
Saturday

3rd ♈

☽ v/c 1:47 am

☽ → ♉ 11:12 am

Color of the Day: Blue
Incense of the Day: Magnolia

Sukkot begins (at sundown on Oct. 2)

Spell For Deeper Sleep and Clearer Dreams

For this spell, mix the following essential oils in equal parts:

* Clary sage

* Lavender

* Marjoram

* Roman chamomile

Before using, test a little of the blend on your skin. If it bothers you, dilute it with a bit of a carrier oil, such as olive or almond. If essential oils aren't available, you can make a hot infused oil (see my spell on July 10 for the technique) with the above herbs.

Next, take a dark blue pillar candle and use a small blade or wooden pick to carve it with symbols and words that represent restful sleep and clear dreams to you. Enhance the look of the candle with silver ink or other decorations. Anoint the candle lightly with the oil, light it safely, and say:

Blessed sleep and revealing dreams

Now ferry me through the night,

To wake aware and full of strength,

To set my life alight!

Meditate for a few moments, then put out the candle. Before lying down, anoint the bottoms of your feet with the oil. May your dreams be blessed.

Thuri Calafia

October 4
Sunday

3rd ♉

Color of the Day: Yellow
Incense of the Day: Frankincense

Find a Tool!

Many of us happily pay for magical bling, but it's equally true that "found" tools and items can be just as wonderful.

Take yourself on a walk to find a tool, whether in a densely wooded area, on an inner-city street, or by the ocean's edge. Leave your electronics in your pocket, and as you walk, open yourself to sensation. Be aware of items, shapes, sounds, or whatever speaks to you. Repeat this mantra:

The world is full of power,
if only I will see.

Is that fallen branch the perfect shape for a wand or bell-branch? Could those peeling pieces of birch bark be pressed, dried, and used as spell-writing paper? Would those herbs, growing wild and fierce through a sidewalk crack, make a powerful magical oil? Could that seashell be used to burn incense? Might those perfectly round stones become a divination tool?

Find your tool, cleanse and charge it, and treasure it forever.

Susan Pesznecker

 October 5
Monday

3rd ♉
☽ v/c 2:41 pm

Color of the Day: Ivory
Incense of the Day: Neroli

Bibliomancy

Close your eyes as you focus on a question and say:

I call upon my higher self to guide
me to the information that is correct
and good for me at this time.

Spend a few minutes in meditation, centering and connecting to your higher self, then select a book from your shelf, allowing intuition to steer your choice. Open the book to a random page, and let your finger fall on a passage. You will do this process three times, flipping to a different page in the book for each selection. Use your intuition to interpret each passage as follows:

Passage 1: *What is the most important thing I can start doing in regard to my situation?*

Passage 2: *What is the most important thing I can stop doing in regard to my situation?*

Passage 3: *What lesson does this situation contain?*

Melissa Tipton

October 6
Tuesday

3rd ♉

☽ → ♊ 12:03 am

Color of the Day: Gray
Incense of the Day: Cinnamon

Taking Out the Garbage (Disposal)

While we don't wish harm on anyone, sometimes we just need to get a bad egg out of our lives. As Kitchen Witches, we like to use things that are readily available in our house for magick, like our garbage disposal.

If there's a person or habit you want out of your life, write their name on a piece of paper and mix it with something you're going to send down the garbage disposal. As you mix the name and the (most likely) old, moldy food, say:

I wish you no harm, but it's time to go away.

Down and gone from me you'll now stay.

I grind and chop up that which doesn't serve me.

The gears have ground and the spell is done. So mote it be!

If you don't have a garbage disposal in your sink, a trash can will work just as well.

Ari & Jason Mankey

October 7
Wednesday

3rd ♊

☽ v/c 9:57 pm

Color of the Day: Yellow
Incense of the Day: Marjoram

New Roads Tarot Spell

Our year will be over at the end of the month. It's time to start thinking about what you want to achieve in the next cycle.

Gather these supplies:

* 5 tarot cards: the four aces and the Sun

* A green candle (for physical manifestation) in a holder

Lay out the tarot cards. Place the Sun card in the middle, with the Ace of Pentacles above it (north/earth), the Ace of Swords to the right (east/air), the Ace of Wands below (south/fire), and the Ace of Cups to the left (west/water). (Note: If you identify swords with fire and wands with air, switch them.) Light the green candle and say:

Ideas meet passion meet creativity meet manifestation. I open myself to new roads of positive abundance and experience. So mote it be.

Spend some time meditating with the lit candle, then extinguish it. Repeat the process for nine days. Be alert to new opportunities and take them.

Cerridwen Iris Shea

October 8
Thursday

3rd ♊

☽ → ♋ 11:45 am

Color of the Day: Purple
Incense of the Day: Balsam

A Stone's Throw Spell

This is the feast day of an obscure saint from Great Britain, Saint Keyne. She's best remembered for her holy enchanted well in England. Wells are magical places. They're portals to the earth and to the underworld. This spell will help rid you of a problem.

First, select a stone you like and hold it tightly. Think of your problem. Walk around a well three times while chanting this charm three times:

The problem I carry with me today,

I forbid to stay.

Go, I demand, be on your way!

At the end of the third chant, toss the stone with force into the well. Don't linger; walk away quickly. If you can't find a well, do the same chant while walking in a circle three times near the edge of a pond or a calm lake.

James Kambos

October 9
Friday

3rd ♋

4th Quarter 8:40 pm

Color of the Day: Rose
Incense of the Day: Violet

Sukkot ends

First Winter harvest

Sukkot, which ends today, is a harvest festival that dates back to the books of Exodus and Leviticus. Today is also the traditional Germanic Winter's Day, for in October the energetic tides of the dark night of the year are getting noticeably stronger. Today is a good day to think about what you might do with your winter.

Place symbols of harvest (perhaps a mini-ear of corn or some wheat) and winter (a crone goddess, amethyst, onyx) on the north side of your altar. Recite this invocation:

Preparing for winter's season today,
I treasure my harvest and look ahead.

Come, dear winter, bring
peace with your holiday,

For we know in time will rise
what once seemed dead.

Speak your wishes for the coming season of rest and regeneration to the crone and keep your symbols on your altar until Imbolc. Use what you learn to welcome whatever winter may bring.

Barbara Ardinger

·October 10
Saturday

4th ♋

☽ v/c 12:04 pm

☽ → ♌ 8:24 pm

Color of the Day: Indigo
Incense of the Day: Pine

World homeless Day

It's World Homeless Day, a day dedicated to reducing homelessness around the world. Today, create a prayer candle for Saint Benedict Joseph Labre, the patron saint of people who are homeless. (After his request to be a monk was refused several times, he released most of his possessions and lived on the streets of Rome. After his death, many miracles were attributed to him.) Print out or create an image of him and paste it onto a jar candle. After lighting the candle, ground and center your energy. Call on Saint Benedict Joseph Labre, and ask for guidance on how you can best help those who are homeless in your area.

While the candle is still burning, research local charities and choose at least one small way to support one of them, perhaps by giving clothing, food, time, or money. Optionally, post your good deed on social media to inspire others to observe this day as well. Extinguish the candle.

Tess Whitehurst

 ·October 11
Sunday

4th ♌

Color of the Day: Orange
Incense of the Day: Hyacinth

Autumn Transitions

Autumn is a season of shift between summer and winter, and nowhere is it easier to see this than in the changes in foliage. Let's use these ideas to help manifest something new this autumn.

Bundle up and go out for a walk. Watch for leaves, looking for those that speak to you. You can approach this as a kind of divination, looking for a leaf that you feel comes with a message, or as a search for a leaf to carry your intention and see it through. Consider that golden leaves could signify wealth or prosperity, orange leaves could reference health or harvest, red leaves could indicate passion or strong emotions, and black or dark leaves might signify anger, danger, or other negativity.

Once home, roll or fold your leaf and secure it with a bit of cotton string. Burn it in a censer or abalone shell, and as it burns, visualize the leaf's intent being realized. Then safely extinguish the flame.

Susan Pesznecker

October 12
Monday

4th ♌

☽ v/c 10:29 am

Color of the Day: Lavender
Incense of the Day: Clary sage

Columbus Day ~
Indigenous Peoples' Day ~
Thanksgiving Day (Canada)

Apple Seed Spell

Apples are often associated with love. They're sweet and filled with juicy good stuff, just like a loving relationship. However, also like relationships, there are little seeds inside an apple that, however small and unthreatening they seem, are actually poisonous and have the potential to grow larger. The seeds are like the small, bitter things that are hidden in an otherwise happy relationship; things like disagreements about chores, petty jealousy, or other annoyances.

If you're finding that your relationship is mostly sweet but those little foibles under the surface are threatening to become big bitter issues, try this apple seed spell.

Gather these materials:

- A bright-red, healthy apple
- A knife
- Twine

Cut the apple in two sideways to reveal the star at its center. The apple represents you and your partner. You fit together perfectly, but between the two of you are these poisonous seeds.

Remove the seeds from the apple one by one. For each seed you remove, name something you'd like to change in your relationship. Place the seeds aside in a pile.

Now put the apple halves back together and wrap them tightly with the twine. This represents that your relationship is intact, with the bitterness removed.

If possible, bury the apple in the ground. Throw the seeds in the garbage and bid them farewell. Be warned: you're probably going to have to discuss these problems now that you've pulled them out into the open, but that's healthy and necessary in a successful relationship.

Kate Freuler

October 13
Tuesday

4th ♌
☽ → ♍ 12:56 am

Color of the Day: Red
Incense of the Day: Geranium

Quick Cash Prosperity Spell

Sometimes we need to perform a working for cash in a hurry. The unexpected happens, bills pile up, and making ends meet is not always an easy task. Cast this spell to summon quick cash.

You will need a green candle in a holder and something to carve it with. On one side of the candle, carve a pyramid, and on the opposite side, carve $¢¢$ (a sigil for success).

Place the candle in a circle of patchouli incense and recite the following spell:

Money, money, come to me,
Come as cash to set me free.

Be here quick and don't delay,
I have bills I have to pay.

By patchouli and green candle,
I summon enough to end this scandal!

Allow the candle to burn all the way down safely on its own.

Devin Hunter

October 14
Wednesday

4th ♍
☽ v/c 6:47 pm

Color of the Day: White
Incense of the Day: Lilac

Cauldron of Annwn Simmer Spell

The Cauldron of Annwn in some myths is said to be the source of inspiration, stirred by nine maidens. Bring some of that inspiration into your home with a fragrant simmer spell with nine ingredients. Gather water, salt, black pepper, cinnamon, nutmeg, lemon, orange, cloves, and rosemary. You can substitute other things you find in your spice cabinet.

Find a sturdy pot and turn your stove on low. Starting with water, add each ingredient one at a time, thinking about what it can bring to your life. (Water nourishes, salt cleanses, pepper awakens, etc.)

Once you have added all nine ingredients, say:

Nine blessings and powers combined,
brought into this home intertwined.

Allow the pot to simmer for an hour or as long as you'd like, but be sure to keep an eye on it and keep enough water in the pot so it doesn't scorch.

Laura Tempest Zakroff

October 15
Thursday

4th ♏

☽ → ♎ 1:54 am

Color of the Day: Turquoise
Incense of the Day: Nutmeg

Freedom from Troubling Thoughts

Even the most loving person can have bad days or experiences where it's difficult to be free from anger, blame, or vengeful thoughts. Whether or not we'd ever give in to such negativity, it's a good idea to gather up that energy, contain it, and neutralize and release it, freeing ourselves from its toxic grip without creating harm.

This time of year is ideal for releasing unhealthy emotions and intentions. For this magic, obtain a stone of any type large enough to fit comfortably in your hand. Squeeze the chosen rock firmly while focusing on all of the problem thoughts. Mentally send them into the rock, visualizing them as dark red-black smoke. When you feel that the transfer is complete, envision the smoke turning a neutral gray. The final step is to take the stone outside and safely toss it away from you, asking that the earth recycle the energy.

Michael Furie

October 16
Friday

4th ♎

New Moon 3:31 pm

☽ v/c 6:11 pm

Color of the Day: Pink
Incense of the Day: Alder

A New Moon Dedication of Witchery

It's officially October, the season of the Witch! Not only that, but it's the new moon (or dark moon) closest to our beloved sabbat of Samhain. Utilize the introspective and emotionally-empowering energies of this new moon to declare yourself a practitioner of the arts.

This evening, venture outside where little light from the city can be seen. Spend some time gazing at the clouds, the stars, and the gorgeous cosmic scene above you. Take some deep breaths in through the nose and out the mouth, inhaling the magickal cosmic energy of the darkened moon. Declare:

I devote myself to you, Great Goddess:
she who guards the mysteries of the
universe; she who comforts the frail;
she whose arms cradle the unknown.
Mighty crone, guard and protect me
on my path, that I learn to harness
my gifts, to honor the earth, to love
and be loved. As I will, so mote it be!

Raven Digitalis

October 17
Saturday

1st ♎

☽ → ♏ 1:05 am

Color of the Day: Black
Incense of the Day: Sage

Querying an Ancestor Spell

If there is an ancestor or other Beloved Dead spirit you feel close to whom you plan to honor this Samhain, either on the holiday itself or with a shrine you've set up for the month, you can ask for their guidance at any time now, as the veil between the worlds becomes gossamer-thin.

For this spell, you simply need a picture or symbol representing the departed spirit and a black candle. Using a small blade or wooden pick, carve your question on the candle, and anoint the candle with some rose or mugwort oil. Place it near the picture of your Beloved Dead and light it safely. Speak to their spirit as you would if they were still incarnate, and tell them you need their help. Ask your question respectfully and give them a deadline to get the answer to you. Thank them from your heart, and let the candle burn all the way down.

In the coming days, stay open to signs and symbols in nature and the words of others, even children, who are often much wiser than we give them credit for.

Thuri Calafia

October 18
Sunday

1st ♏

☽ v/c 5:43 pm

Color of the Day: Yellow
Incense of the Day: Almond

Putting the Earth to Bed

Each year as the weather cools and the plants start to wither, we need to put the earth to bed. The earth needs to rest and repair so that it can give again in the spring.

Tend to the yard one last time, making sure that leaves are raked up and fallen branches are cleared. Return plant matter to the garden, and till it one last time. If you have compost or other soil to mix in, now is the time to add it to the earth. Give thanks for the bounty that was received, and as you turn the last shovel of earth, say:

Now to rest you go, and again in the spring you will sow.

Charlynn Walls

October 19
Monday

1st ♏

☽ → ♐ 12:43 am

Color of the Day: White
Incense of the Day: Narcissus

When You're at a Crossroads

Everyone has free will, and not even the angels can take it away. But sometimes it's hard to know what outcome is best. When you're stuck between two choices, this spell will help you make the decision. Remember, you've always got the right to change your mind! You'll need two saucers, a bottle of spring water, and the tops cut off two carrots.

Fill the saucers with water, and place one carrot top in each. Set them in a light, dry place, somewhere fairly warm and where you'll see them often. Keep them topped up with water from the bottle. Envision one carrot being one path and the second carrot being the other option. The carrot top that sprouts first and grows the strongest is the right path for you to take in this instance.

Charlie Rainbow Wolf

October 20
Tuesday

1st ♐

☽ v/c 11:38 pm

Color of the Day: Black
Incense of the Day: Ylang-ylang

Release Your Burdens

When you feel like you're carrying a heavy burden or otherwise need to let go of dense, stuck energy, go for a walk and look for a stone that's hefty but light enough for you to safely pick it up. Ask the stone if it would be willing to remove some of your heavy energy, and if you intuitively get a green light, proceed with the spell.

Holding the rock in both hands, bring to mind your burden, and allow any thoughts and emotions to arise. When you feel ready, send the burdensome energy into the stone, and once the transfer is complete, hold the stone aloft and drop it to the ground from waist height or higher. (Watch your toes!) Feel the lightness following the stone's release and notice any shifts in your energy. Thank the stone for its aid.

Melissa Tipton

October 21
Wednesday

1st ♏ ♐

☽ → ♑ 2:44 am

Color of the Day: Topaz
Incense of the Day: Honeysuckle

Five Points of the Apple and You

Apples are not only one of our favorite fruits but also great magickal tools. Cut an apple in half across its middle (not through the stem) and notice the pentagram (five-pointed star) that's now visible. The five points of the star correspond to the five centers of the body. Cut five slices from your apple and then eat each one to magickally fortify the five different parts of you.

The first slice represents the brain and the logic that guides our daily lives. The second is for the emotions that shape us. The third is for our bodies and the motion they create. The fourth is for the instincts that keep us safe and push us into action. The fifth is for the passions and love that connect us to those we care about. As you eat each slice of the apple, think about these things and how they are functioning in your life.

Ari & Jason Mankey

NOTES:

October 22
Thursday

1st ♑

☉ → ♏ 7:00 pm

Color of the Day: Purple
Incense of the Day: Mulberry

Remove a Ghost Spell

If you have a ghost in your house, follow these instructions in the following verse to rid yourself of your resident spirit.

*When the sky is cloaked in
the black of deepest night,*

Light a virgin candle, tall and white.

*Place it by a mirror, gaze until the
image is no longer your own,*

*Say quietly, "Come, spirit, let
me show you the way home."*

*Walk out into the night, carry
the candle in your hand,*

*Urge the spirit to move on
its way to Summerland.*

*As the clock strikes midnight
and the winds begin to roar,*

*Feast the spirit, place an
apple by your door.*

*The next morn, bury the
apple in an earthly plot,*

*Leave it be, let it spoil, let
it decay, let it rot.*

*May your mind be at ease,
you treated the spirit well,*

*It has traveled on to Summerland,
and so ends this spell.*

James Kambos

October 23
Friday

1st ♑

☽ v/c 12:35 am

☽ → ♒ 8:17 am

2nd Quarter 9:23 am

Color of the Day: White
Incense of the Day: Mint

hearth and happiness
Cleaning Spell

The holidays are almost upon us, stretching from Samhain through Twelfth Night. Before you start all that holiday cooking, it's time to clean the kitchen!

Light some jar candles and put on some music. Invoke Hestia, Rosmerta, and the Kitchen God. Use your favorite green cleaners and floor washes, or a mixture of vinegar and baking soda (don't lean over it; it bubbles), and get to work. Sing at the top of your lungs as you scrub your heart out.

Clean the oven, wash the stove and the countertops, clean out the cupboards, toss expired food, wash the floors, change the curtains, polish the fixtures, dust the cookbooks, and polish silverware, candlesticks, and copper pots.

Maybe even set up a shelf altar for a hearth spirit, and remember to say thanks each time you prepare a meal!

Cerridwen Iris Shea

 October 24
Saturday

2nd ♒

☽ v/c 5:54 pm

Color of the Day: Gray
Incense of the Day: Rue

Fall Cleaning

Spring cleaning gets a lot of press, but fall cleaning makes just as much sense. After all, in many parts of the Northern Hemisphere, we're shutting our windows and getting ready to camp out at home for winter and the holidays, so of course we want to create a clean, cozy, organized, and energetically positive space for the months ahead.

Today, diffuse cinnamon and clove essential oils as you give your home a good, thorough cleaning. If you have time, you might also want to clear clutter and tackle some of the cleaning projects you haven't gotten to for a while. Finish by lighting a stick of cedar incense, holding it over a dish or plate and giving the entire home a light yet powerful smudge. Move through each room and area in a clockwise direction with the smoke to bless the home with harmony, clarity, protection, energy, and health.

Tess Whitehurst

October 25
Sunday

2nd ♒

☽ → ♓ 5:18 pm

Color of the Day: Gold
Incense of the Day: Juniper

A Nearing hallow's household Blessing

To bless your home throughout the tide of autumn, consider burning some sticks of your favorite all-natural incense. For this working, it's best to burn quite a lot all at once; the more smoke the better—just be sure to be mindful of your fire alarms!

Light a few orange or black candles in holders to celebrate the season. As you burn your chosen sacred smoke, walk throughout your home and open every cupboard and closet. Waft the smoke in every space, and while doing so, repeat:

Cleansed and purified,
enchanted and sanctified.

Follow in suit by saying the same affirmation while sprinkling salt water with your fingertips.

If you wish, walk around your house or apartment building in a deosil (clockwise) fashion to bless the outside perimeter. Don't forget to bless your Halloween decorations too!

Raven Digitalis

October 26
Monday

2nd ♓

Color of the Day: Silver
Incense of the Day: Rosemary

Sweet Words Spell

Every day we deal with people with whom we just can't seem to communicate for some reason. We simply don't vibe with certain individuals, and no matter how hard we try, our words always seem to come out wrong, causing awkward or upsetting results. If this keeps happening to you, try this spell.

Place your lip balm or gloss in a bowl of sugar. Place your hands over the bowl and envision your words flowing from your lips eloquently, communicating perfectly what you'd like to say. See the result of your words causing the recipient to smile in response. Feel the understanding blossoming between the two of you. Cover the bowl of sugar with a cloth and leave it overnight.

The next day, put on your lip gloss like always and try to set things right. Dispose of the sugar, or use it in your coffee, tea, or baking to bring more sweetness to you.

Kate Freuler

October 27
Tuesday

2nd ♓

☽ v/c 8:46 pm

Color of the Day: Scarlet
Incense of the Day: Ginger

No Fear!

Put together a miniature "brave kit" so you'll always be prepared to deal with frightening or malevolent forces.

You'll need:

- A small hinged tin (the kind breath mints come in)
- Salt
- Flash paper
- A white tealight candle and holder
- Matches in a waterproof container
- Small stones or crystals (fluorite, obsidian, and amethyst are ideal)
- Charged water (i.e., water that has been charged in the light of the sun or the full moon)
- A small piece of soft fabric
- A small "golf" pencil
- 1 or 2 iron nails
- Small vials with screw-on lids (for the water and salt)

Fit the items into the tin box. You're now prepared for a variety of spells and conjures. Cast a circle with the salt, write spells on flash paper and cast/ignite them into being, work candle magic, set up a small altar on the fabric, asperge an area with water, use the iron nails for protection against negative energy, and so forth.

Susan Pesznecker

October 28
Wednesday

2nd ♓

☽ → ♈ 4:45 am

Color of the Day: White
Incense of the Day: Bay laurel

Glamour Spell

Last night, Venus entered Libra, a sign that embodies this planet's hunger for beauty and attention. Cast this spell on yourself so that everyone who sees you will find some aspect of you absolutely desirable. All you need is a pink candle in a holder and something to carve it with.

Using your carving tool, etch the symbol of Venus (♀) into one side of the candle, and the symbol for Libra (♎) into the other. On the bottom of the candle, etch your initials. Light the candle, then cover your eyes and say:

See no ugliness, see no fear,
see only what you hold dear.

Cover your ears and say:

Hear no wickedness, hear no lies,
listen only to what sounds wise.

Lastly, put your hands a few inches in front of your mouth and say:

Speak only flattery, taste only sweet,
give me your attention from head to feet!

Let the candle burn out safely on its own.

Devin Hunter

October 29
Thursday

2nd ♈

Color of the Day: Crimson
Incense of the Day: Carnation

To Commune with Your Ancestors

This is the season when the veil between our world and other realities is thinnest, making it the perfect time to reach out to and visit with your ancestors. Their blood courses through your veins; you're already bonded. This spell strengthens those ties. You'll need a pen and paper, catnip, rose petals, a heatproof surface, and a lilac-colored candle and something to light it with.

Write down the names of the ancestors you wish to remember. Sprinkle the catnip and rose petals on the heatproof surface. Place the candle on top and light it. Gaze into the flame, and read out the name of the person(s) you'd like to spend time with. Focus on the light of the candle binding you together. Feel their DNA in you as you sit in the glow of the flame. When you're finished, pinch out the candle, but leave it on the herbs, with the list of names next to it, until November 3.

Charlie Rainbow Wolf

October 30
Friday

2nd ♈

☽ v/c 12:12 pm

☽ → ♉ 5:19 pm

Color of the Day: Purple
Incense of the Day: Yarrow

Flush and Be Gone!

J ust before the Samhain festivities begin, a simple banishing of troublesome little things could be in order. This is a great time to get rid of unnecessary things so that we enter the dark time ready to begin a fresh cycle with a minimum of distractions.

An easy, effective, at-home banishing can be done with a few easily obtainable things: a felt-tip marker and some toilet paper. Write what you wish to be rid of on pieces of toilet paper while visualizing being free of these things. Crumple up each piece of paper individually and toss it in the toilet. Flush them away, and as you do so, say:

Unbind and release, flush and be gone; obstacles banished, the battle is won.

From unneeded burdens, I now break free; into the future I travel with ease.

Michael Furie

October 31
Saturday

2nd ♉

🌕 Full Moon 10:49 am

Color of the Day: Brown
Incense of the Day: Patchouli

Samhain – Halloween

Blue Moon

T his Samhain night is also a blue moon, which is the second full moon of any month. Gather your circle for a Samhain blue moon ritual tonight. Prepare tokens that symbolize good fortune. (If you plan far enough ahead, you can collect wishbones and paint them with blue glitter.) Ask your priestess du jour to dress like the Blue Fairy in Disney's *Pinocchio* and lead everyone in a meditation to find out what wishes their hearts make. At the end of the meditation, the Blue Fairy can give everyone a glittery wishbone or a piece of blue lace agate and this magical verse written in blue ink on the palest blue paper:

On this night when the moon is blue, I hear your wish and make it true!

—xoxoxox

—The Blue Fairy

Go around the circle telling what your wishes are. Figure out practical ways to help them come true.

Barbara Ardinger

November

The sounds of nature begin to quiet down in November, but this month is far from silent. Yes, the cheery morning birdsong of spring is gone, and crickets are no longer fiddling on warm summer afternoons, but November has its own "voices." On a frosty November morning, you'll hear a faint, faraway gabble. Raise your eyes toward the sky, and coming over the horizon, in a V formation heading south, is a flock of wild geese. The sound makes you pause and wonder: how do they know it's time to migrate? As you rake leaves, the late autumn breeze stirs them, and they softly rustle as they click and swirl up the street. Few sounds say November like the wind. It may be as gentle as a baby's breath or it may roar, carrying the weight of the coming winter as it howls in the night. During the night you can also hear November's most haunting voice: the lone hooting of an owl. Yes, this month has many voices, but every evening I hear the most comforting voice of all. That voice belongs to the crackling of burning logs as my hearth fire wards off the chill of a dark November night.

During this mysterious month, let the voices of November speak to you, igniting your imagination and your magic.

James Kambos

November 1
Sunday

3rd ♉

☽ v/c 9:29 pm

Color of the Day: Orange
Incense of the Day: Eucalyptus

All Saints' Day –
Daylight Saving Time
ends at 2:00 a.m.

honoring the Mighty Dead

Those who have crossed the veil before us deserve to be honored, especially at this time of year.

Gather photos and representations of your deceased loved ones, and lovingly set them on an altar. Decorate the shrine with offerings of candles, food, drink, grains, toys, and anything the deceased enjoyed while incarnated on the earth plane.

Talk and communicate with each of the beloved dead individually. As you do so, discuss their positive qualities and write them on a piece of paper. Continue doing this for all ancestors on the shrine so that you are left with a piece of paper filled with positive qualities that you wish to embody in your own life. Thank the deceased for their work on this planet. Pin this magickal paper next to your bedside so you can meditate on these positive qualities every day, further invoking them into your life.

Raven Digitalis

November 2
Monday

3rd ♉

☽ → ♊ 5:00 am

Color of the Day: White
Incense of the Day: Lily

All Souls' Day Blessing

Pagans seem to think that the word *soul* is the private property of the standard-brand religions. For a thousand years, however, soul, which is not a Latin word and comes from the Teutonic *sáwl* and the Gothic *saiwala*, has meant "the principle of life in humans or animals." Linguists tell us that in English the most basic words are the Anglo-Saxon ones; *soul* is thus an idea basic to our knowledge of ourselves.

Although All Souls' Day was created to bring the dead through Purgatory, that's not one of our articles of faith. Let us instead pray for and bless all the dead people we see on the news so that they may rest awhile and then be reborn into brighter, safer new lives:

Rest now, and sleep in peace,

Forget the terror, bombs, and wars.

*When you wake in that
unknown other place,*

*Release old lessons, set out
for morning stars.*

Barbara Ardinger

November 3
Tuesday

3rd ♊

Color of the Day: Black
Incense of the Day: Basil

Election Day (general)

Make It Right, Make It Right

This is a spell to help correct an error, whether political, personal, or global. Gather these items:

- 2 candles (one black, one white) with holders
- Olive oil
- A cauldron (or heatproof bowl)
- A wand
- A representation of the problem (a photograph, drawing, etc.)

Anoint both candles from each end to the middle with the oil. On a table, place the black candle to the left and the white one to the right, with the cauldron between them and the wand in front of the cauldron so its handle faces away from you, the tip pointing toward you. Place the representation of the problem between the wand and you. Light the candles, building a strong visualization of your goal. Pick up the wand and slowly, with inten-sity, turn it forward so the tip points to the cauldron, and say:

> Out of balance, chaos reigned;
> shifting now to corrected course.
>
> Reversing harm, the error wanes;
> restored and mended, by magical force.

Extinguish the candles and burn the representation in the cauldron.

Michael Furie

November 4
Wednesday

3rd ♊

☽ v/c 8:49 am

☽ → ♋ 4:45 pm

Color of the Day: Yellow
Incense of the Day: Lavender

Find Your Courage

We'd all like to believe that life is going to be easy. If that were the case, it would be called "perfection," not "life"! There are always going to be upsets—but you can't focus on the negativity. Finding your strength and integrity when things go wrong is how you grow your soul. For this spell, you'll need some tobacco, a piece of red cotton or wool cloth, and a length of red cotton or wool yarn or string. Use natural fibers, not synthetic.

Wrap the tobacco up in the cloth, then tie it shut with the yarn. Put this in your pocket, carry it in your purse, or even put it in an amulet pouch and wear it as a talisman. It will help you find the courage to face your challenges in a strong and positive manner, and remind you that there's nothing you and your divinity can't handle.

Charlie Rainbow Wolf

 November 5
Thursday

3rd ♋

Color of the Day: Turquoise
Incense of the Day: Myrrh

Four Thieves Vinegar

The legend of four thieves vinegar tells of four thieves who each contributed to a vinegar mixture, drank it together, and survived a local plague. Your own four thieves vinegar will be useful for all kinds of spellwork.

You'll need:

- 4 of your favorite fragrant or fiery herbs or spices (such as allspice, cayenne, cinnamon, dried peppers, peppercorns, rosemary, sage, tarragon, etc.)
- 1 cup vinegar
- 1 pint-size Mason jar
- 5 garlic cloves

Crush or break the hard peppers and spices. Chop the herbs. Pour the vinegar into the Mason jar.

Slice each garlic clove in half and add to the jar. As you do this, intone:

Earth, air, fire, water, spirit.

Add your four chosen additions, then screw on the lid and shake. Store out of direct light, shaking once a day. In five days, it's ready to use.

Use your vinegar to dress candles, add to potions, sprinkle in smudges, bless tools, or for almost any purpose. Sprinkle around the boundary of your home for protection.

Susan Pesznecker

November 6
Friday

3rd ♋

☽ v/c 8:27 pm

Color of the Day: Pink
Incense of the Day: Orchid

World Day to Protect the Environment in War

So many of us care dearly about the wellness of our beloved Mother Earth, and so many of us deplore war in all forms and constantly wish for peace. But we don't often talk about the grievous harm war does to our planet. Today is a day for both concerns: the United Nations named today the World Day to Protect the Environment in War. (Its technical but less catchy name is the International Day for Preventing the Exploitation of the Environment in War and Armed Conflict.)

Today, light a blue or white candle for Eirene, the Greek goddess of peace. In addition to being the embodiment of peace, she has an earthy aspect, as she is often pictured with a cornucopia, ears of corn, or the baby Plutus (the divine child of the Eleusinian mysteries), indicating that with peace comes the ability to tend to the earth, and therefore prosperity for all. (Be sure to extinguish the candle.)

Tess Whitehurst

November 7
Saturday

3rd ♋

☽ → ♌ 2:18 am

Color of the Day: Blue
Incense of the Day: Sandalwood

Ancestors Acknowledgment

This an ideal time to connect with ancestors and other loved ones who have crossed over. You can send messages to them and receive them too!

If there is someone specific you wish to connect with, write them a short note or letter on paper, addressing them directly. Before going to bed, fold the paper up, and set fire to it in your cauldron, along with a pleasing incense. Address that ancestor by name, saying:

> _____, I greet you and send
> you blessings from this realm
> to yours. If it pleases you, send
> return greetings in my dreams.

Pay careful attention to your dreams in the next three days to receive their answer.

Laura Tempest Zakroff

 November 8
Sunday

3rd ♌

4th Quarter 8:46 am

Color of the Day: Amber
Incense of the Day: Heliotrope

Cleansing Citrus

This spell can be performed once as needed, or repeat it each morning for a week to intensify the effects. You'll need the juice of a fresh lemon, preferably organic, and a glass of water (cold or hot, your choice). Stir the two together as you say:

> Lemon, as I start my day,
>
> Increase my health,
>
> Keep harm at bay.
>
> Cleanse my body, mind, and soul,
>
> And let no evil take its toll.

Enjoy your lemon water, and feel the cleansing, protective energy infuse your entire body and aura, lending a brightness and clarity to your mind and mood and dissolving any harmful or unneeded energy.

Melissa Tipton

November 9
Monday

4th ♌
☽ v/c 6:05 am
☽ → ♍ 8:30 am

Color of the Day: Silver
Incense of the Day: Hyssop

Blowing Leaves Spell

Gather some fallen leaves from a nearby tree and set them aside somewhere to dry. Once they are dry, take some paint and a small paintbrush (a pen will most likely break the leaf) and write on the leaves anything you'd like to get rid of in your life. This could be a bad habit, a toxic relationship, or an unwanted guest.

On a blustery day, take your leaves outside to a local park and throw them up in the air, saying:

*Winds of the east, take this
burden away from me.*

*Spirits of air, let me be
truly and happily free.*

*As I weave my spell,
I say so mote it be!*

The wind should take your leaves, and with them, the burdens you are trying to get rid of in your life. If the leaves don't blow away immediately, don't worry. They will eventually.

Ari & Jason Mankey

 November 10
Tuesday

4th ♍

Color of the Day: Maroon
Incense of the Day: Cedar

Headache Release Spell

Today honors Áed mac Bricc, an Irish saint who died in 589 CE. He is the patron saint of headache sufferers. There's a story from the sixth century that says he healed Brigit of her headache—because even a goddess of smithing, healing, and poetry should have someone to ease her headache.

Today, safely burn lavender-scented candles, put rosemary oil on your temples, and soak in a lavender-scented bath. Carve time out of your day to relax, release your tense muscles, and call on Áed mac Bricc to remove your headache. Then extinguish the candles.

If you're lucky enough to be headache-free today, soak and light candles and ask him to remove a future headache, banking the healing to draw on when you need it.

Cerridwen Iris Shea

November 11
Wednesday

4th ♏︎

☽ v/c 5:58 am

☽ → ♎︎ 11:09 am

Color of the Day: Brown
Incense of the Day: Marjoram

Veterans Day –
Remembrance Day (Canada)

Spirit Guide Spell

Happy Veterans Day! If you're in the US, be sure to thank a veteran for their service and sacrifice today. Today also happens to be 11/11, an auspicious day for those who work with the magic of synchronicity. Working with our spirit guides is a powerful way to discern synchronicity, and today is the perfect day to make a pact with them to check in daily. Today at 11:11 a.m. or p.m., reach out to your spirit guides and recite:

Better angel or spirit guide,
from you I will not hide.

At 11:11, let us meet,
a daily check-in to complete.

From this, our bond shall grow,
and your better I shall know!

Every day after, when the clock strikes 11:11, reach out to your spirit guides. When you see 11/11 on your own, see that as a reminder from them to check in.

Devin Hunter

November 12
Thursday

4th ♎︎

Color of the Day: Crimson
Incense of the Day: Clove

A Thursday to Relax

In many places, November is gloomy and chilly. Today's a good day to stay indoors and cozy up with your beloveds, both human and feline or canine. Read a good book to them.

Le Petit Prince, by Antoine de Saint-Exupéry, is supposed to be a children's story. *Le renard,* the fox, asks the little prince to "tame" (make friends with) him. The fox gives the little prince (and us) an important life lesson when he says, *On ne voit bien qu'avec le coeur. L'essentiel est invisible pour les yeux.* ["It is only with our hearts that we can truly see. What is essential is invisible to the eyes."]

Set figures or drawings of people and animals that have tamed you on your altar. See them with your heart. See the essence of each relationship and draw a picture of it or set a symbol of it on your altar. Do a ritual whose intention is gratitude.

Barbara Ardinger

November 13
Friday

4th ♍︎ ♎︎
☽ v/c 6:32 am
☽ → ♏︎ 11:19 am
Color of the Day: White
Incense of the Day: Rose

The Gift of Giving

The Roman festival of Feronia is recognized today. Feronia was a goddess of fertility, abundance, and prosperity. She was also known to take on a disguise and ask for help from others. Those who did so were well rewarded, but those who did not…well, they didn't fare so well.

To tap into the spirit of abundance and prosperity on this day, find a small way to give back to others. Take a much-loved object and donate it or give it to someone you feel would treasure it. Before you gift the item, hold it in your hands and say:

May you be blessed,
May all you hope for be addressed.

Once the item is charged, give it away and know you will also be blessed by your actions.

Charlynn Walls

November 14
Saturday

4th ♏︎
Color of the Day: Black
Incense of the Day: Magnolia

Divining with Smoke

To see the future, try this old-time method of divining with smoke. You'll need:

• Some dried chrysanthemum petals or foliage, crumbled

• 1 whole clove, crushed

• A bit of cinnamon stick, grated

Begin a small fire in a heatproof container. Then sprinkle the dried herbs over the flames. As the smoke begins to rise, say this charm:

With these herbs crumbled fine,

Let me see the future
that shall be mine.

Smoke: breathe, curl, and rise,

Let my fate be revealed before my eyes.

Be open to all images you see in the rising smoke. If you wish, record them in a journal. Watch the smoke for no more than ten minutes at first. The next time you can gaze longer. Let the fire go out. When the ashes are cool, discard them outside by sprinkling them on the earth.

James Kambos

November 15
Sunday

4th ♏

New Moon 12:07 am

☽ v/c 6:13 am

☽ → ♐ 10:47 am

Color of the Day: Gold
Incense of the Day: Marigold

New Moon Stone

It's a new moon! Time for fresh beginnings and starting projects. Make a new moon stone to absorb this refreshing energy and boost your activities. This is also a good way to shake off procrastination and get an endeavor off the ground.

Find a dark-colored stone that fits in the palm of your hand. It can be a fancy crystal or just a smooth rock you find. Take it outdoors on the night of the new moon and hold it up to the sky. Imagine the energy of the new moon beaming into the stone, filling it up with hopeful, energetic light. Leave it outdoors for the night and then collect it in the morning.

Keep your new moon stone with the materials for any burgeoning projects that need a kickoff. If you're an artist, keep it with your paints. If you want to build something, keep it with your tools. Then get to work!

Kate Freuler

November 16
Monday

1st ♐

Color of the Day: Gray
Incense of the Day: Narcissus

True Friend Spell

Sometimes the approaching holidays can make us feel a little lonely, particularly if our friends are busy or if they aren't meeting our needs as well as we'd like. It might be time to add some more people to our circle of friends.

For this spell, take a medium-size clear quartz crystal and hold it in your right hand. Think about what a great friend you are—be honest with yourself about all your good qualities. When you feel that the crystal is full of your authenticity and promise, hold it up above your head and visualize a bright spotlight of energy bursting forth from it into the night sky, beckoning to those who would be the best friends for you. Chant:

I'm sending up a beacon

To pierce the darkest night.

Come see how awesome I can be!

Behold my shining light!

When the power peaks, open yourself to the feeling of having many friends who all love you truly and wish to spend time with you.

Thuri Calafia

♥ November 17
Tuesday

1st ♐

☽ v/c 2:55 am

☽ → ♑ 11:35 am

Color of the Day: Red

Incense of the Day: Ylang-ylang

Celebrate Romance Spell

Taking a moment to acknowledge a relationship that is going strong can be a wonderful way to honor that partnership. For this spell, gather these items:

- A bowl of rose petals (dry or fresh)
- 2 white tealight candles in holders
- A lighter or matches

Sitting with your partner, hold the bowl of rose petals out to them so they can dip their hands in and rub the petals between their fingers. Then have them hold the bowl for you as you do the same. Set the bowl down, and smell the aroma on each other.

Next, each of you hold a candle and have the other light it for you. Place the candles on the table (or floor) between you, with about four to six feet of space in between. Together, take petals from the bowl and sprinkle them around the candles, forming a figure eight. Then look into each other's eyes for a count of six breaths.

Laura Tempest Zakroff

▽ November 18
Wednesday

1st ♑

Color of the Day: Topaz

Incense of the Day: Lilac

Underwater Bathtime Balancing

To connect more deeply with the essence of water, thereby connecting to your own emotional healing and awareness, draw a bath. Sit with the water in dark silence, listening to the sounds of the flowing fountain filling the tub with life-giving water. The sound may put you into a sort of trance; allow this to happen.

Next, add essential oils, bath salts, etc. Slip into the tub and rock your body slightly to feel the tides of the water coming and going. Again, allow yourself to become entranced by the mystical nature of this element. Bring to mind the qualities of water; consider how precious this resource truly is. Offer your gratitude.

When you're ready, totally submerge your head in the water. When you do this, "shout" various terms underwater that link you to the element in positive ways, for example, *purified, cleansed, nourished, rejuvenated,* or *empathetic.* Use your creativity to enchant the water and yourself by yelling underwater. Quite appropriately, you will be the only one able to hear these sacred shouts.

Raven Digitalis

November 19
Thursday

1st ♑

☽ v/c 11:30 am

☽ → ♒ 3:25 pm

Color of the Day: Purple
Incense of the Day: Jasmine

A Servant's Hands

At this time of year, as we move into what many celebrate as a season of giving, it's a good time to work magic over ideals of service and altruism.

Wash your hands before you begin, using a favorite soap and drying with a clean towel. Admire your hands, envisioning their strength, experience, and wisdom.

Using a piece of white paper, write down the great works your hands have done. Perhaps they've knit sweaters to keep people warm, cooked meals to nourish others, played music, nursed people back to health, tilled gardens, or even built houses. Now list the volunteer efforts you'll carry out in the coming year.

Fold this paper and tuck it into a journal or a corner of your altar space so it's available to review. Anoint your hands with a favorite lotion or a dab of oil, repeating:

May these hands, so able and
strong, give help to others,
through seasons long.

Susan Pesznecker

November 20
Friday

1st ♒

☽ v/c 7:49 pm

Color of the Day: Rose
Incense of the Day: Cypress

happy holidays

With Thanksgiving less than a week away, the holiday season is well and truly upon us. The conditions are perfect today for working magic for a happy holiday season, particularly for fostering respect amid varying viewpoints and promoting the paradigm of forgiveness, acceptance, and love.

Brew a small pot of Earl Grey tea. Sweeten a cup with honey and place it on your altar for Concordia, the Roman goddess who was traditionally invoked to heal family and marital discord. Sweeten another cup of tea with honey for yourself. Sit before your altar and petition Concordia by saying:

Great Goddess Concordia, may
this holiday season be filled with
sweetness, friendship, and love.
Please open my heart and the hearts
of my friends and family. Please
protect us from drama. Please bless
all our gatherings with harmony,
respect, and happiness. Thank you.

Enjoy your tea, then take the offering outside and pour it upon the earth.

Tess Whitehurst

November 21
Saturday

1st ♒

☉ → ♐ 3:40 pm

☽ → ♓ 11:06 pm

2nd Quarter 11:45 pm

Color of the Day: Brown
Incense of the Day: Rue

Change as a Blessing

Here's a way to spread some cheer. You'll need some coins, a bowl of salt water, and some time.

If possible, buy a roll of quarters for this spell, although any coins or paper money will do. If using coins, soak them overnight in the bowl of salt water, then rinse and dry them. This step cleanses them psychically and physically. If using paper money, dab salt water on the corners of each bill, then allow them to dry. Once the coins or bills are cleansed and dried, hold your hands over them and visualize pure light pouring into the money, charging it with the magic of blessing. When you're ready, say:

Valuable money I cleanse and
release, to those who need
blessings and joy and peace.

Whoever shall find these
gifts I share, good luck and
happiness will then be theirs.

Leave the money on shelves in stores or just about anywhere for people to find.

Michael Furie

November 22
Sunday

2nd ♓

Color of the Day: Orange
Incense of the Day: Frankincense

A Gratitude Spell

In many areas, this is the season when the last of the harvest is gathered, and feasting on the produce takes place. The quickest path to abundance is one of gratitude. For this spell, you'll need a plate full of your favorite foods.

Take a bite of food, and speak out loud what you're thankful for. Keep doing this until you've eaten a sufficient amount. Leave a bit of extra food on your plate, and take it outside to offer it to the universe. Like energy always attracts like energy.

If you feast with others in a celebration of thanksgiving, you can take turns expressing your thanks and gratitude. Writing your thoughts down so you can reflect on them when the going gets tough is a good idea too.

Charlie Rainbow Wolf

November 23
Monday

2nd ♓

Color of the Day: Lavender
Incense of the Day: Rosemary

Courage Before Family Oil

The holiday season often means spending time with family members we might not get along with, which can cause a lot of anxiety. For a little extra courage, add the following to a small vial of olive oil (or other carrier oil):

- 1 whole clove
- A pinch of basil
- A dash of oregano
- 1 almond sliver

Dab the oil on your wrists when faced with unpleasant or stressful situations. The vial should be small enough to fit in your pocket easily and discreetly so it can be used as needed, and the scents from the oil will complement a family meal and not attract any undue attention.

Ari & Jason Mankey

November 24
Tuesday

2nd ♓

☽ v/c 5:44 am
☽ → ♈ 10:05 am

Color of the Day: Scarlet
Incense of the Day: Geranium

Safe Holiday Travels Spell

With the holiday season coming up, it's a good idea to make a small amulet to protect you on your travels. Gather these supplies:

- An amethyst
- Rosemary
- A dollar coin
- A small black bag

Bless and consecrate your supplies. Speak the following as you drop each item into the bag:

Amethyst for protection and clarity,

Rosemary for protection and love,

A coin for protection and prosperity.

I am blessed in my travels.

So mote it be.

Carry this bag with you when you travel. Keep it on your altar when you're at home. Boost the spell on the night before each journey by holding it in your hand and repeating:

I am blessed in my travels.

So mote it be.

Cerridwen Iris Shea

November 25
Wednesday

2nd ♈

Color of the Day: White
Incense of the Day: Bay Laurel

The Color of Harmony

Use this spell when you're experiencing relationship disharmony and you want to shift the energy in a more productive direction.

You'll need two glasses of water and two shades of food coloring. Choose colors that produce a pleasing color when mixed, like yellow + blue (green), red + yellow (orange), or blue + red (purple). The glasses do not represent the people in this situation; they represent qualities being expressed and goals that are currently at odds.

Place a few drops of each color in separate glasses. Bring the relationship dynamic to mind, and place your left hand over one glass and your right over the other as you say:

Left and right, black and white, I call upon the power of polarity to bring healing and balance to this relationship. The qualities that stand at odds are harmonized according to the highest good, harming none.

Pour the glasses one into the other, then back and forth, blending the opposing qualities into a vibrant, beautiful new color.

Melissa Tipton

November 26
Thursday

2nd ♈

☽ v/c 6:46 pm
☽ → ♉ 10:43 pm

Color of the Day: Green
Incense of the Day: Nutmeg

Thanksgiving Day

Reconnecting Through Food

Today in the United States is Thanksgiving Day. This is a day for feasting, families, and gratitude. As such, it's an excellent time to do a little kitchen magick to bolster your connections and relationships. Whether you are creating your own feast or contributing a dish, you can do a little spell during its creation.

As you are preparing the food, you can stir it clockwise, or if making dough, you can speak the following words while kneading it:

Let this food nourish,
May our connection flourish.

This will link you to all that partake of your offering and help to bolster the relationships that you currently have.

Charlynn Walls

November 27
Friday

2nd ♉

Color of the Day: Coral
Incense of the Day: Thyme

Black Friday Get the Deal Spell

It's the day after Thanksgiving, which means that all hell is about to break loose in the world of retail shopping! If you plan to do any bargain hunting today, cast this spell before going out to ensure that you get the best deals.

You will need the Six of Coins (Pentacles) card from your favorite tarot deck. Hold the card in your hand and recite this spell:

Saving money is what I need,
by Six of Coins I will succeed.

Bring me discounts and a deal,
when I show them, they'll say it's a steal.

All obstruction out of my way,
I am the master of Black Friday!

Put the card in your pocket, purse, or wallet and shop!

Devin Hunter

November 28
Saturday

2nd ♉

Color of the Day: Blue
Incense of the Day: Ivy

A November Wind Spell

Now the November wind begins to blow winter our way. This is a good time to use the force of the wind to end a problem in your life. If possible, perform this spell on a windy night. You'll need a black candle in a holder, paper, pen, and a heatproof container.

Light the candle and write your problem on the paper. Concentrate on ending your problem. Then carefully ignite the paper by holding it to the flame. Let it burn out in the container. Immediately blow out the candle. When the ashes cool, take them outside to scatter. It would be perfect if you're able to take them to an isolated crossroads, but your backyard is fine. Scatter the ashes, then say:

The wild November wind
blows with an icy blast.

My problem shall end, let
it fade into the past.

End the spell by throwing the candle away. Soon you'll notice your problem begin to lessen.

James Kambos

November 29
Sunday

2nd ♉

☽ v/c 7:48 am

☽ → ♊ 11:16 am

Color of the Day: Yellow
Incense of the Day: Almond

Guiding Eye Spell

This spell is for when you're unsure of which direction to take in any aspect of your life and need some spiritual guidance.

Gather these materials:

• A white candle in a holder

• A 3 x 3-inch slip of paper

• 1 whole dried bay leaf

• A marker that is the same color as your eyes

• A pin

Light the candle and write these words on the paper:

Spirit, show me the way. Open my eyes to opportunity and joy. So mote it be.

Notice that when a bay leaf is placed sideways, it's the shape of a human eye. Draw an iris and pupil on the leaf with a marker that is the same color as your own eyes. Then, using the pin, gently poke a hole in the center to represent the pupil opening and being able to see.

Place the leaf on the paper. Using your white candle, carefully drip a thin layer of wax over the leaf and paper, binding them. Hide this flat charm inside your phone case so it's always with you.

Kate Freuler

☾ November 30
Monday

2nd ♊

Full Moon 4:30 am

☽ v/c 11:22 pm

Color of the Day: Ivory
Incense of the Day: Neroli

Lunar Eclipse

Cyber Monday Prosperity Spell

With Spending Too Much Season well under way at this point, some of us may wish to curb our enthusiasm a bit in order to keep a roof over our heads!

For this spell, you'll need your wallet and some prosperity herbs (such as almond or patchouli) combined with some herbs of protection (such as bay leaves or mint). Mint is especially good for this spell, as it has properties of both prosperity and protection. You'll also need to inscribe and anoint a green candle by carving symbols and words into it with a small blade or wooden pick and dressing it with a simple oil, such as olive or a scented oil (such as patchouli). Then sprinkle your altar with some coins and bills.

Breathe deeply and visualize yourself finishing any holiday shopping you need to do, smiling broadly because you've hit sales and found bargains so that you've been able to hold on to a lot of your hard-earned money. Light the candle safely and sprinkle the money with the herbs. Say:

The gods reward my generosity in kind. I have more than enough.

Put the money and herbs in your wallet, and extinguish the candle. Whenever you spend this holiday season, repeat these words again and again to yourself.

Thuri Calafia

December

D ecember features a palette of cool colors: white snow, silver icicles, evergreen, and, of course, blue—the bright cerulean sky on a clear, cold winter's day, or the deep navy velvet of the darkening nights, culminating on the longest night of the year, the winter solstice. This hue is reflected in December's birthstones: turquoise, zircon, tanzanite, and lapis. The notion of a stone representing each month has been linked to ayurvedic beliefs that suggest correspondences between the planets and crystals. It wasn't until the eighteenth century that associating stones with a birth month became a popular practice in the Western world.

Even if you weren't born in December, you can still tap into the power of this month's special stones. Zircon increases bone stability, which is good for moving over icy terrain. Use turquoise, a rain-making stone, to summon snow. Turquoise also heals and brings peace. Engage tanzanite's powers for psychic visions for the impending new year. Lapis—the mirror of the winter night sky, and a stone that can be found in the breastplate of the high priest—brings wisdom and awareness.

Natalie Zaman

December 1
Tuesday

3rd ♊

☽ → ♋ 10:33 pm

Color of the Day: Black
Incense of the Day: Ginger

Bring the Light Spell

As the nights get longer, it's important to remember the light and bring it into your home. Acquire a tall white pillar candle. If it's one that is already in glass, grab a marker to write on the glass with. If it's an all-wax candle, find a safe holder for it, and you can write directly into the wax, using a toothpick or ballpoint pen.

Make six asterisks (*) around the sides of the candle, plus one large asterisk across the top, with the wick at the center. Light the candle (and remake the top asterisk as necessary), saying:

Light of sun and twinkle of star,

Make your way here from afar.

Into this home, bring your light,

Holding back the dark of night.

Laura Tempest Zakroff

December 2
Wednesday

3rd ♋

Color of the Day: Yellow
Incense of the Day: Lavender

Shiva Meditation

Today is sacred to the Lord of the Dance, who is portrayed as standing on one foot inside a rayed circle, dancing his cosmic dance of life-death-rebirth. Shiva, whose name means "benevolent" or "favorable," is a pre-Aryan god. His consort is Parvati, who is also Sita, Uma, and Durga.

We are not cultural pirates and we don't want to steal the gods and practices of other faiths. But we can learn from them. Go outside today and gaze at what the dance of the seasons looks like where you live. Go outside again tonight and look up into the sky and imagine the dances of the planets and stars.

Now go inside where it's warm and cast a circle and begin your own dance. Even if you can't "really" dance, move in ways that remind you of Shiva's cosmic dance and its place in your life. Dance for your life.

Barbara Ardinger

December 3
Thursday

3rd ♋

Color of the Day: White
Incense of the Day: Apricot

Krampus holiday Fun Spell

Krampus is the original "wild man" of the Yuletide season. Though he has a reputation for being a rather stern figure, he's usually the life of the party.

If the holidays have you depressed, place a small piece of mistletoe in a bag (mistletoe is poisonous, so keep it wrapped up!) and say the following words over it:

May I be merry,

May I be bright,

Never contrary,

A Yuletide delight.

Krampus, hear my plea.

This is my will, let it be!

The powers of Krampus and the mistletoe will help you overcome any holiday malaise and make you the center of attention at any office Christmas party.

Ari & Jason Mankey

NOTES:

December 4
Friday

3rd ♋

☽ v/c 5:29 am

☽ → ♌ 7:53 am

Color of the Day: Purple
Incense of the Day: Alder

helping hands

This spell is useful for projects that require a sustained effort, from a few days to a few years. You'll activate five powers, one for each of your fingers. Throughout the project, you can call on any or all of these powers when needed by pressing together the relevant fingers and bringing the power to mind:

- *Thumb:* Strength; the ability to gather and apply energy in service of your goal

- *Index finger:* Focus; mindful attention on aspects relevant to your goal

- *Middle finger:* Balance; effective interplay of polarities, such as work/rest, intellect/intuition, etc.

- *Ring finger:* Commitment; sustained effort and motivation for the duration of the project

- *Pinkie:* Creativity; the ability to think and do in new ways and make interesting, relevant connections

To activate the powers, press the fingers of the opposite hands together, one at a time, as you say:

> *I activate the powers at hand:*
>
> *The strength of the thumb,*
>
> *Focus of the index,*
>
> *Balance of the middle,*
>
> *Commitment of the ring,*
>
> *And creativity of the pinkie.*

Melissa Tipton

December 5
Saturday

3rd ♌

☽ v/c 5:28 pm

Color of the Day: Gray
Incense of the Day: Sage

Saint Nicholas Day Fun

This is an old family tradition in our house, based on the European tale of Saint Nicholas coming this night to fill the shoes/stockings of the household (one of the origins of the Santa tales). We decided to keep it and incorporate it into our pagan rituals. Saint Nicholas Day is actually tomorrow, but tonight is the fun.

Before bedtime, each individual in the house puts out a shoe, either at the hearth or outside their bedroom door.

When it's quiet, household members sneak out and fill each other's shoes with favorite chocolates, fruit, bags of chocolate coins, and a small toy. Part of the fun is not being caught by other household members!

Before you distribute the items, make sure you bless them, giving thanks to Saint Nicholas for his generosity.

Everyone finds a shoe filled with delightful treats in the morning!

Cerridwen Iris Shea

December 6
Sunday

3rd ♌

☽ → ♍ 2:46 pm

Color of the Day: Orange
Incense of the Day: Marigold

Cleansing Bell

Spiritual cleansing of the home is often done with smoke, smudging or misting an area to clear away unwanted vibrations. Did you know this can also be achieved by using sound? Next time you're in a thrift store, see if you can find a small hand-held bell. These are often made of brass or other metals, and make a resonating, clanging noise when you shake them.

Cleanse your bell in the moonlight, then carry it around your home. In each room, ring the bell as hard and loud as you can, and see the sound vibrations filling the space, pushing away all stale and unwanted energy. Imagine the sounds of the bell filling every nook and cranny of each room with the clear, bright vibration, permeating every inch of your space and neutralizing it.

This cleansing method is a good alternative for those who don't like smoke or heavily scented products.

Kate Freuler

December 7
Monday

3rd ♍
4th Quarter 7:37 pm

Color of the Day: Silver
Incense of the Day: Clary sage

Deep Sleep

Winter's long, dark nights can support our sleep, which benefits every aspect of our mental and physical health. Like flower bulbs beneath the cold winter soil, winter rest helps us replenish our energy before the more expansive months of spring and summer.

To support deep and restful sleep, cleanse a black tourmaline in bright sunlight, sage smoke, or running water. At bedtime, hold it in your right hand and sense its calming, grounding vibrations moving through your entire physical body, all the way to your toes, your fingers, and the crown of your head. Feel your muscles release and notice that you are safely cocooned in the crystal's protective energy.

Continue to hold the crystal in your hand (or otherwise close to your body) as you sleep, tonight and any other night that you'd like to support your sleep. During the day, set the crystal on a bright windowsill to cleanse and recharge it in the sun.

Tess Whitehurst

December 8
Tuesday

4th ♍
☽ v/c 5:35 pm
☽ → ♎ 7:01 pm

Color of the Day: Scarlet
Incense of the Day: Bayberry

Peace Be with You

The holidays are so stressful for some folks. Maybe there's a lot to do and not enough time to do it. Perhaps you're alone, or maybe you've got a large and argumentative family. Whatever the situation, this spell will help you keep your cool and find a way to stay peaceful and centered. You'll need a pen and some unlined paper, a candle in a holder, and something to light it with.

Write down the names of the people who stress you out—or, if it's a situation and not a person, write that down. Draw a circle around what you wrote, and place it under the candle. Light the candle, and as you do so, say:

Peace around me,

Peace before me,

Peace between me and thee,

So mote it be.

If you can let the candle burn down on its own safely, do that. If not, pinch it out.

Charlie Rainbow Wolf

December 9
Wednesday

4th ♎

Color of the Day: White
Incense of the Day: Honeysuckle

Snow Writing

Do you need a creative boost? This is a great time to harness the energy of the season. The weather has usually turned cold by now, and snow is often in abundance.

If you are able to stand or sit outside, do so. See if you can differentiate between the individual flakes of snow. Each one is unique and has its own structure. Find a spot that has been previously undisturbed. If there isn't one or if you don't have any snow, you can shave some ice to achieve the same effect.

What kind of creative boost do you need? Write it in the snow and say:

Ideas come to me so that I can manifest them into being.

Leave the message in the snow and let it slowly dissipate.

Charlynn Walls

December 10
Thursday

4th ♎

☽ v/c 7:56 pm
☽ → ♏ 8:59 pm

Color of the Day: Crimson
Incense of the Day: Myrrh

Human Rights Protection Spell

Today is Human Rights Day, the anniversary of the release of the Universal Declaration of Human Rights, which contains thirty articles and outlines the basic rights granted to every person regardless of their origin or economic status. These rights are threatened every day and deserve our protection. This isn't always easy to do when you don't know how to help. Cast this spell to lend strength to those working to free themselves from these abuses.

Take a black candle and hold it in your hands, then say:

*There may not be much that
I can do, but with this candle
I lend my light to you.*

*You are not forgotten, you are not lost,
you shall be protected at all costs!*

*Your rights have been violated,
and that is not okay, I summon
the angels to drive evil away!*

Light the candle in a holder and place it near a window until it burns out. Donate to a human rights organization.

Devin Hunter

December 11
Friday

4th ♏

Color of the Day: Coral

Incense of the Day: Vanilla

hanukkah begins (at sundown on Dec. 10)

A holiday Spending Spell

Here's a spell to help keep your holiday spending under control. You'll need a dollar bill, a cinnamon stick, and some gray ribbon or yarn. You'll also need about two days for this spell to begin working.

First, select a night and hide the dollar bill outside your front door. The next morning, bring it in and wrap it around the cinnamon stick. Secure the dollar to the cinnamon stick by tying it into place using the ribbon or yarn; tie it in a knot. Next—this is important—don't spend any money today. Visualize your money growing. See yourself spending just what you need for gifts. Place the dollar, still tied to the cinnamon stick, in your pocket or purse. Carry it with you as you shop for gifts. If you get the urge to overspend, touch the dollar until the feeling passes. This will keep you from splurging.

James Kambos

▽ **December 12**
Saturday

4th ♏

☽ v/c 8:58 pm

☽ → ♐ 9:39 pm

Color of the Day: Indigo

Incense of the Day: Pine

Elixir of Light

To make this elixir, you will need the following ingredients:

- 2 cups fresh cranberries, washed and finely ground
- 1 quart-size Mason jar
- Shaved peel of an orange
- 1 cup sugar
- Vodka

Add the cranberries to the Mason jar and top with the shaved orange peel and sugar. Fill the jar with vodka, adding it slowly and topping it off over the next few hours as the liquid sifts through the fruit and sugar mixture. Cap, shake, and set aside.

Allow the elixir to age—gathering strength—on the countertop for six weeks, shaking it daily. It should mostly stay out of direct light, but if possible, allow it to charge in both moonlight and full sun for a few hours.

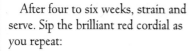

After four to six weeks, strain and serve. Sip the brilliant red cordial as you repeat:

> Berries bright as little suns,
>
> Jewels sweet in winter's eye,
>
> Fill me now with quiet strength,
>
> Sharp against the dark of night.

Feel the cordial filling you with warmth, vigor, and energy!

Susan Pesznecker

December 13
Sunday

4th ♐

Color of the Day: Gold
Incense of the Day: Heliotrope

Saint Lucy's Day (and Night)

Lucina was an early Italian goddess of light who became an aspect of Juno or Diana. Saint Lucy was a fourth-century Sicilian girl who consecrated her virginity to God and was martyred. Vikings liked the stories they heard about Lucy while they were conquering Sicily and northern Italy and took them home. Before the calendar was reformed, Lucy's feast day was the longest night of the year. People lit Lucy candles and Lucy fires, which guided the sun back to the sky, and children wrote the word *Lussi* on fences, walls, and doors to inform the demons of winter and darkness that their reign was ended.

Do your own Lucy's Night ritual with your circle by safely lighting many candles and shining the light into all possible dark corners, real and imagined. Laugh and play and recite this silly rhyme:

> Lucy, Lucy, shining bright,
>
> Banish all the shadows of the night.

Barbara Ardinger

December 14
Monday

4th ♐

☽ v/c 11:17 am

New Moon 11:17 am

☽ → ♑ 10:35 pm

Color of the Day: White
Incense of the Day: Lily

Solar Eclipse

Dissolving the Stress

There are times when things seem overwhelming and we just need to rest and take the pressure off. Holiday time is usually chaotic even in the best of circumstances, but this day is also a new moon/solar eclipse in Sagittarius, so the frenzy might be at its peak. If you feel overwhelmed and in need of a break, try this quick magical technique.

If possible, burning frankincense or rosemary incense helps to enhance this work. Find a quiet place to sit and close your eyes. Envision a thin strand of light coming down from above and going straight through your body. Feel the light begin to expand, bathing and surrounding your whole body in silver-blue light. Sense this light cleansing you of any anxiety or stress. Now visualize that the light forms a protective mirrored shell around you to keep further stress at bay. It is done.

Michael Furie

December 15
Tuesday

1st ♑

Color of the Day: Maroon
Incense of the Day: Cedar

honor an Ancestor

Maintaining an active, loving relationship with a deceased grandparent or other ancestor is a wonderful spiritual practice, and both parties (you and the ancestor) benefit. A simple but powerful way to do this is by having a dedicated ancestor altar somewhere in your space. This could be as simple as a candle placed near a framed photo, but you could also add incense, flowers, items that used to belong to the ancestor, food or drinks they enjoyed during life, perfume or soap they used to use, or anything else that reminds you of them.

Light the candle regularly as you connect with the ancestor's spirit. The more you do this, the more available this loved one will be to help guide you, support you, and send luck and blessings your way from the other side, often in ways hilariously similar to the ways they used to help and support you during life.

Tess Whitehurst

December 16
Wednesday

1st ♑

Color of the Day: Brown
Incense of the Day: Bay laurel

Step Into Your Beauty Spell

The holiday season can be especially challenging at times as we hustle and bustle to get it all done. The upcoming company parties and family gatherings all call for us to be at our best, but often what we really want is just one evening to relax and enjoy some peace. For this spell, you'll need to take that evening. Force yourself!

First, run yourself a nice hot bath and throw a pinch of salt, a squeeze of lemon, and a few rose petals into the water. Allow yourself a nice long soak while contemplating your "flaws." Pull the plug and let the water drain away before you get up. Say:

> My perceived flaws are
> nothing but dross; cultural
> constructs I no longer need.

Stand up and say:

> I am perfect and wonderful just
> as I am, for the gods made me.

Anoint your chakras with rose oil, if desired, repeating the above phrase.

Thuri Calafia

December 17
Thursday

1st ♑

☽ v/c 12:34 am

☽ → ♒ 1:27 am

Color of the Day: Turquoise
Incense of the Day: Clove

Breaking Free

For this spell, you'll need a slip of paper, a pen, and a handful of salt or sand. Choose a decision or situation in which you feel stuck, and write a concise description of it on the paper. Place the paper on a table, and ring it with a circle of sand or salt, making sure there are no gaps. Spend a few moments feeling into this stuckness, noticing where it appears in your body and any thoughts or images that arise. When you feel ready to shift, say:

> This stuckness that has held me tight,
>
> I cast aside with all my might.
>
> New options, ways, ideas appear,
>
> The path ahead is free and clear!

Break open the circle of salt/sand with your fingers and feel the energy shift, then journal or meditate in this space to receive guidance on your next empowered action step. Rip up the paper and throw it away, along with the sand/salt.

Melissa Tipton

December 18
Friday

1st ♒

Color of the Day: Rose
Incense of the Day: Rose

hanukkah ends

Peace and Love Spell

December 18 marks the end of Hanukkah, and with Yule and Christmas on the way, it's the perfect day to celebrate our bonds and similarities as faith communities and human beings. For this spell, you'll need five candles of any color in holders. As you light each candle, say one of the following lines and reflect on the connections and promise we have as human beings.

For the bonds we share as humans.

*For the gods both known
and unknown.*

For the seasons we all share together.

For the promise of a brighter tomorrow.

*For the love we should all
share with one another.*

After the candles are all lit, take a deep breath and reflect on the things we have in common with each other instead of our differences. Resolve to do what you can to make the world a better place and to celebrate our similarities. Extinguish the candles. Blessed be.

Ari & Jason Mankey

December 19
Saturday

1st ♒

☽ v/c 3:45 am

☽ → ♓ 7:39 am

Color of the Day: Black
Incense of the Day: Sandalwood

Spell for Patience

The holidays are often stressful on multiple levels. Every old hurt can come forward and rip open. It's a good time to perform a patience spell. You will need a pink candle in a holder, rose oil, and a small rose quartz. Bless and consecrate your supplies. Anoint the candle and yourself with the oil. Light the candle.

Follow your breath and focus softly on the candle flame. Hold the rose quartz in your hands. Attune to your heart. Feel yourself fill with peaceful, patient energy. Imagine a filter around your heart that screens out and disposes of any harmful words, gestures, or energy sent your way but allows friendship, joy, and goodwill to enter. Imagine any negativity sent your way bouncing off like rain on an umbrella.

Ground yourself by standing with both feet on the ground and imagining any excess energy flowing into the earth. Take a deep breath to center. Be sure to extinguish the candle or let it burn down. Carry the rose quartz with you throughout the holidays.

Cerridwen Iris Shea

December 20
Sunday

1st ♓

Color of the Day: Yellow
Incense of the Day: Juniper

Prosperity Sachet

For this spell, you will need the following items:

- A piece of green cloth
- A green marker
- Coins
- Pine needles
- Cinnamon or cloves
- Green ribbon

Find a quiet space where you'll be undisturbed, with your items laid out before you. Envision yourself receiving money, either by imagining your bank account numbers going up or by visualizing a wad of cash in your hand. While you do this, draw a money sign ($) on the cloth with the marker, then write your name beneath the sign.

Hold all the other items in your hands, and see yourself living prosperously. Feel the relief of being debt-free, the rush of being able to pay bills with ease, and maybe even the joy of owning some nice things you wish you could buy. Place the items in the center of the cloth, then tie the edges tight with the ribbon, forming a little bag. As you knot the ribbon, say:

Prosperity comes to me, so mote it be.

Hang the sachet somewhere near your front door to welcome the prosperous energies.

Kate Freuler

December 21
Monday

1st ♓

☉ → ♑ 5:02 am

☽ v/c 5:25 am

☽ → ♈ 5:32 pm

2nd Quarter 6:41 pm

Color of the Day: Gray
Incense of the Day: Hyssop

Yule – Winter Solstice

Yule Log Blessing

Blessed Yule! Traditionally, a Yule log was burned as a symbol of the old, dark year being reborn as the fresh new cycle in the form of radiant, sparkling flames. To make this tradition your own, find yourself a nice, old log (nothing from a live tree) that will burn safely in your fireplace or fire pit. (Customarily, the log was oak.) To thank and honor the old year, anoint the log with essential oil of frankincense. To bless the new cycle and to fill it with sweetness, abundance, and luck, anoint the log with essential oil of cinnamon. (Be careful not to get any on your skin.) Place the log in the fireplace or fire pit and say:

Farewell to the old and welcome the new,
Heartfelt thanks for blessings true.

We honor now this sacred night,
When deepest darkness births the light.

Light the log and feel the magic.

Tess Whitehurst

December 22
Tuesday

2nd ♈

Color of the Day: Red
Incense of the Day: Ylang-ylang

A Peace Candle Spell

This candle spell is good to use any time, but it's very helpful during the holiday season. Perform this spell before you have company, preferably a day or two ahead of time. It's ideal to use if you'll be entertaining relatives who don't get along. You'll need two white or blue candles, olive oil, and a white or blue piece of fabric.

First, rub each candle with a drop of olive oil. Visualize your guests enjoying themselves. Then wrap the candles in the fabric. Put the candles in a quiet place, such as a closet, for a day or two. This will let them magically charge.

Before company arrives, place the candles where your guests will sit. Safely light the candles. As they burn, "see" their flames surrounding your guests with peace and calm.

James Kambos

December 23
Wednesday

2nd ♈

☽ v/c 5:51 pm

Color of the Day: Topaz
Incense of the Day: Lilac

A Nameless Day with huge Potential

The Celtic tree calendar has one day that exists outside of the calendar, as it does not belong to a particular tree. It is sometimes referred to as the "nameless day." Due to the nature of this day, which is not tied to anything, it has limitless potential. Today is a great day to manifest your dreams into reality.

Take a piece of printer paper and place it in front of you. Through this paper, you can see that the possibilities are limitless. You can write, draw, or fold this paper, transforming it into countless new creations.

Take a few moments to think about what you want to manifest in your life. Then mark or fold the paper in front of you to make visible what you have only thought of before. Place this paper in a place where you can see it daily.

Charlynn Walls

December 24
Thursday

2nd ♈

☽ → ♉ 5:55 am

Color of the Day: Purple
Incense of the Day: Apricot

Christmas Eve

Celebrating the Magic of Winter

Whether you celebrate Christmas or not, you can still do this spell. You'll need a two-piece clear plastic ornament. If you can't get one, an empty clear plastic bottle will do. You'll also need a selection of small, inexpensive items that represent what is important to you. Buttons from Grandma's button jar, petals from your favorite flower, brightly colored yarn and thread, and colored pebbles are just a few options. I'm sure you can think of many more!

Put these items in the ornament (or bottle), and with each one you place, consider what gift it represents in your life. When the ornament (or bottle) is full, close it up and hang it on your tree, or place it outside on a tree branch or fence post. See it as a reminder of everything that is good and right in your life, because like energy always attracts like energy.

Charlie Rainbow Wolf

December 25
Friday

2nd ♉

Color of the Day: Pink
Incense of the Day: Cypress

Christmas Day

Pinecones Aplenty Spell

At this time of year when we often give gifts to each other, don't forget the wildlife, especially if snow covers much of the ground.

If you have pinecones where you live, gather some up and acquire some honey and birdseed. Affix a wire or sturdy string to the pinecone so you can both handle and hang it. Roll the pinecone in honey and then generously through the seeds, then let it set. Think:

A gift from me to all of you, so you may see the winter through.

Now take the pinecone outside and affix it to a fence, pole, or tree branch so the birds and other critters may enjoy the treat. Replenish as necessary.

Laura Tempest Zakroff

December 26
Saturday

2nd ♉

☽ v/c 6:32 am

☽ → ♊ 6:33 pm

Color of the Day: Blue
Incense of the Day: Patchouli

Kwanzaa begins ~
Boxing Day (Canada & UK)

Celebrate Community

Kwanzaa is a seven-day holiday honoring African-American culture and community. You can observe this celebration with your own mini-festival. If possible, do this with family and friends, for the real point of Kwanzaa is community.

You'll need an item to represent each of Kwanzaa's seven principles:

First night: Unity (an example of what I might use: a family photo)

Second night: Self-determination (a diploma)

Third night: Collective responsibility (two cords knotted together)

Fourth night: Cooperative economics (several coins)

Fifth night: Purpose (my planning journal)

Sixth night: Creativity (a sketch)

Seventh night: Faith (a piece of magical jewelry)

Festoon your altar with red, gold, green, and brown cloths, and add a chalice (filled with your celebratory drink of choice) and a brightly colored candle and holder.

Each evening, light the candle, place that evening's item on the altar, and speak of that night's principle. Share stories and ideas. Finish with drinks from the chalice and share your plan to take the Kwanzaa principles to heart. Then extinguish the candle.

Susan Pesznecker

December 27
Sunday

2nd ♊

Color of the Day: Gold
Incense of the Day: Almond

honor What's Old

We've come nearly to the end of the year, to its midnight, to its eldest days. Everything seems old, old, old. This is the season of the crone, of the hag. *Hag* comes from *hagia* and means "holy." The hag is the Holy One. In Northern Europe, hags, called *volvas*, were sibyls; an important Icelandic text is the *Voluspa*, "Sibyl's Vision." Thanks to the aging of the baby boom generation, we meet crones and sages every day.

Cast your circle and set your altar with gold, silver, and purple candles in holders, plus symbols of the stages of your life so far. Find your favorite agates (representing strength, courage, and longevity) in your collection and set them in the center. Using a feather, wave the energies of the candles toward yourself. Extinguish the candles.

Keep the agates on your altar and carry an agate in your pocket. Be kind to older citizens who may need some help sometimes.

Barbara Ardinger

December 28
Monday

2nd ♊

☽ v/c 10:01 pm

Color of the Day: Ivory
Incense of the Day: Neroli

hear My Voice Spell

Saturn recently entered the sign of Aquarius, ushering in a time when our social values and norms will be forced to adapt to the changing times. This is an excellent time for those who have been marginalized in the past to have their voices heard and to have a real impact on society. If you are a member of a marginalized group, use the energy of the day to finally get your voice heard.

You will need the Judgment card from the tarot. Hold the card in your hands and visualize yourself inside the scene. See the change you seek happen right before your eyes, then say:

Hear the call from above,
fly in peace like a dove.

Stay and meet the changing tide, or
meet wrath from which you can't hide.

Tomorrow shall come from
what we do today, I call upon
judgment to open the way!

Put the card on your altar and visit it often.

Devin hunter

December 29
Tuesday

2nd ♊

☽ → ♋ 5:28 am

Full Moon 10:28 pm

Color of the Day: Gray
Incense of the Day: Cinnamon

Full Moon

As stated in Doreen Valiente's classic Wiccan Rede, "When the moon rides at her peak, then your heart's desire seek."

Now that the sun is beginning to return to earth following the winter solstice, it's a good time to weave your wishes into reality. If you live in a snowy or cold area of the world, it may feel like the sun will never return. But have no fear: the seasons always change, and we grow both older and wiser with the passing of each year.

In many cultures, the moon represents that subtle internal wisdom that keeps families, communities, and homes tied together with a loving bond. Considering these aspects in your own life, weave your wishes for the year by writing these goals on a small, smooth wooden log or board.

In the spirit of a Yule log, safely kindle a fire and set the log alight while performing any additional magick for these goals that you see fit. You may even wish to make this a crafty project for the whole family or coven!

Raven Digitalis

December 30
Wednesday

3rd ♋

Color of the Day: Yellow
Incense of the Day: Marjoram

Multipurpose Candle Spell

A good basic candle spell is a magical must-have. The easiest candles to work with are votives and chimes. They're small and readily available. Choose a candle color that aligns with your goal: red for love, green or gold for money, black for protection, etc.

Once you have your candle, hold it tightly in your dominant hand, mentally willing your desire into the wax. When it feels fully charged, anoint the candle with your saliva to seal the intention. You can write your desire on a slip of paper to be set underneath the candle holder.

Place the candle in a holder and light it, saying:

To reach my goal, this spell ensure;
power of flame, release my desire.

This energy now I summon
and stir, the magic is poured
out through the fire.

For highest good, manifest for
me; as I will, so mote it be.

Extinguish the candle.

Michael Furie

December 31
Thursday

3rd ♋

☽ v/c 8:45 am

☽ → ♌ 1:58 pm

Color of the Day: White
Incense of the Day: Balsam

New Year's Eve

New Calendar Eve Spell

We made it! The old calendar is about to be yanked from the wall and a new calendar hung up to mark the passing of the days. The moon is just past full, so it's a good time to release that old year!

For this spell, take that old calendar to your altar, along with a few colorful markers. Even though, as a Witch, you've long since marked the new year on the great Wheel, you recognize that this symbol in your hands still holds a lot of power. So page through those days, remembering all that you learned, and mark the calendar with tears, laughter, anger, joy, pain. Let it all out. Express yourself!

Then, if you can do so, carefully burn the calendar or shred it by hand, saying:

I let the past go in peace. I'm ready
to face 2021 and all its lessons.

Be blessed.

Thuri Calafia

Daily Magical Influences

Each day is ruled by a planet that possesses specific magical influences:

Monday (Moon): peace, healing, caring, psychic awareness, purification.

Tuesday (Mars): passion, sex, courage, aggression, protection.

Wednesday (Mercury): conscious mind, study, travel, divination, wisdom.

Thursday (Jupiter): expansion, money, prosperity, generosity.

Friday (Venus): love, friendship, reconciliation, beauty.

Saturday (Saturn): longevity, exorcism, endings, homes, houses.

Sunday (Sun): healing, spirituality, success, strength, protection.

Lunar Phases

The lunar phase is important in determining best times for magic.

The waxing moon (from the new moon to the full moon) is the ideal time for magic to draw things toward you.

The full moon is the time of greatest power.

The waning moon (from the full moon to the new moon) is a time for study, meditation, and little magical work (except magic designed to banish harmful energies).

Astrological Symbols

The Sun	☉	Aries	♈
The Moon	☽	Taurus	♉
Mercury	☿	Gemini	♊
Venus	♀	Cancer	♋
Mars	♂	Leo	♌
Jupiter	♃	Virgo	♍
Saturn	♄	Libra	♎
Uranus	♅	Scorpio	♏
Neptune	♆	Sagittarius	♐
Pluto	♇	Capricorn	♑
		Aquarius	♒
		Pisces	♓

The Moon's Sign

The moon's sign is a traditional consideration for astrologers. The moon continuously moves through each sign in the zodiac, from Aries to Pisces. The moon influences the sign it inhabits, creating different energies that affect our daily lives.

Aries: Good for starting things but lacks staying power. Things occur rapidly but quickly pass. People tend to be argumentative and assertive.

Taurus: Things begun now do last, tend to increase in value, and become hard to alter. Brings out an appreciation for beauty and sensory experience.

Gemini: Things begun now are easily changed by outside influence. Time for shortcuts, communications, games, and fun.

Cancer: Stimulates emotional rapport between people. Pinpoints need, supports growth and nurturance. Tend to domestic concerns.

Leo: Draws emphasis to the self, to central ideas or institutions, away from connections with others and emotional needs. People tend to be melodramatic.

Virgo: Favors accomplishment of details and commands from higher up. Focus on health, hygiene, and daily schedules.

Libra: Favors cooperation, compromise, social activities, beautification of surroundings, balance, and partnership.

Scorpio: Increases awareness of psychic power. Favors activities requiring intensity and focus. People tend to brood and become secretive under this moon sign.

Sagittarius: Encourages flights of imagination and confidence. This moon sign is adventurous, philosophical, and athletic. Favors expansion and growth.

Capricorn: Develops strong structure. Focus on traditions, responsibilities, and obligations. A good time to set boundaries and rules.

Aquarius: Rebellious energy. Time to break habits and make abrupt change. Personal freedom and individuality are the focus.

Pisces: The focus is on dreaming, nostalgia, intuition, and psychic impressions. A good time for spiritual or philanthropic activities.

Glossary of Magical Terms

Altar: A table that holds magical tools as a focus for spell workings.

Athame: A ritual knife used to direct personal power during workings or to symbolically draw diagrams in a spell. It is rarely, if ever, used for actual physical cutting.

Aura: An invisible energy field surrounding a person. The aura can change color depending on the state of the individual.

Balefire: A fire lit for magical purposes, usually outdoors.

Casting a circle: The process of drawing a circle around oneself to seal out unfriendly influences and raise magical power. It is the first step in a spell.

Censer: An incense burner. Traditionally a censer is a metal container, filled with incense, that is swung on the end of a chain.

Censing: The process of burning incense to spiritually cleanse an object.

Centering yourself: To prepare for a magical rite by calming and centering all of your personal energy.

Chakra: One of the seven centers of spiritual energy in the human body, according to the philosophy of yoga.

Charging: To infuse an object with magical power.

Circle of protection: A circle cast to protect oneself from unfriendly influences.

Crystals: Quartz or other stones that store cleansing or protective energies.

Deosil: Clockwise movement, symbolic of life and positive energies.

Deva: A divine being according to Hindu beliefs; a devil or evil spirit according to Zoroastrianism.

Direct/retrograde: Refers to the motion of a planet when seen from the earth. A planet is "direct" when it appears to be moving forward from the point of view of a person on the earth. It is "retrograde" when it appears to be moving backward.

Dowsing: To use a divining rod to search for a thing, usually water or minerals.

Dowsing pendulum: A long cord with a coin or gem at one end. The pattern of its swing is used to answer questions.

Dryad: A tree spirit or forest guardian.

Fey: An archaic term for a magical spirit or a fairylike being.

Gris-gris: A small bag containing charms, herbs, stones, and other items to draw energy, luck, love, or prosperity to the wearer.

Mantra: A sacred chant used in Hindu tradition to embody the divinity invoked; it is said to possess deep magical power.

Needfire: A ceremonial fire kindled at dawn on major Wiccan holidays. It was traditionally used to light all other household fires.

Pentagram: A symbolically protective five-pointed star with one point upward.

Power hand: The dominant hand; the hand used most often.

Scry: To predict the future by gazing at or into an object such as a crystal ball or pool of water.

Second sight: The psychic power or ability to foresee the future.

Sigil: A personal seal or symbol.

Smudge/smudge stick: To spiritually cleanse an object by waving smoke over and around it. A smudge stick is a bundle of several incense sticks.

Wand: A stick or rod used for casting circles and as a focus for magical power.

Widdershins: Counterclockwise movement, symbolic of negative magical purposes, sometimes used to disperse negative energies.

About the Authors

Barbara Ardinger, PhD (www.barbaraardinger.com), is the author of *Secret Lives*, a novel about a circle of crones, mothers, and maidens, plus goddesses, a talking cat, and the Green Man. Her earlier books include the daybook *Pagan Every Day*, *Goddess Meditations*, *Finding New Goddesses* (a parody of goddess encyclopedias), and *Quicksilver Moon* (a realistic novel…except for the vampire). She is also well known for the rituals she creates. Her day job is freelance editing for people who have good ideas but don't want to embarrass themselves in print. Barbara lives in Southern California with her two rescued cats, Heisenberg and Schroedinger.

Thuri Calafia is an ordained minister, Wiccan High Priestess, teacher, and author of *Dedicant: A Witch's Circle of Fire* and *Initiate: A Witch's Circle of Water*. Currently, she is working on her third book, *Adept: A Witch's Circle of Earth*. She lives in the Pacific Northwest with her beloved Labrador, Briana Fae.

Raven Digitalis (Missoula, MT) is the author of *Esoteric Empathy*, *The Everyday Empath*, *Shadow Magick Compendium*, *Planetary Spells & Rituals*, and *Goth Craft*, all from Llewellyn. He is the cofounder of a nonprofit multicultural temple called Opus Aima Obscuræ (OAO), which primarily observes Neopagan and Hindu traditions. Raven has been an earth-based practitioner since 1999, a Priest since 2003, a Freemason since 2012, and an empath all of his life. He holds a degree in anthropology from the University of Montana and is also a professional Tarot reader, DJ, small-scale farmer, and animal rights advocate.

Kate Freuler lives in Ontario, Canada, with her husband and daughter. She owns and operates www.whitemoonwitchcraft.com, an online witchcraft boutique. When she isn't crafting spells and amulets for clients or herself, she loves to write, paint, read, draw, and create.

Michael Furie (Northern California) is the author of *Supermarket Sabbats*, *Spellcasting for Beginners*, *Supermarket Magic*, *Spellcasting: Beyond the Basics*, and more, all from Llewellyn. A practicing Witch for more than twenty years, he is a priest of the Cailleach. He can be found online at www.michaelfurie.com.

Devin Hunter (San Francisco Bay Area) is a bestselling author who holds initiations in multiple spiritual, occult, and esoteric traditions and is the founder of his own tradition, Sacred Fires, and cofounder of its offshoot community, Black Rose Witchcraft. His podcast, *The Modern Witch*, has

helped thousands of people from all over the world empower themselves and discover their psychic and magical abilities. Devin is the co-owner of the Mystic Dream, a metaphysical store in Walnut Creek, CA, where he offers professional services as a medium and occultist.

James Kambos learned about charms and folk magic from his Greek grandmother and mother. He's a writer and an artist who designs cards. He holds a degree in history and geography from Ohio University and lives in the beautiful hill country of southern Ohio.

Ari Mankey has been practicing Witchcraft and creating spells for over twenty years. Away from the Craft, she has devoted her life to medical laboratory science and developing the perfect whisky ice cream.

Jason Mankey has written five books for Llewellyn and is a frequent speaker and teacher at Pagan festivals across North America. He lives in Northern California with his wife, Ari, where they run two local covens.

Susan Pesznecker is a mother, writer, nurse, college English professor, and Baden-Powell Service Association scout and lives in the beautiful Pacific Northwest with her poodles. An initiated Druid, green magick devotee, and amateur herbalist, Sue loves reading, writing, cooking, travel, camping, swimming, stargazing, and anything having to do with the outdoors. Her previous books include *Crafting Magick with Pen and Ink*, *The Magickal Retreat: Making Time for Solitude, Intention & Rejuvenation*, and *Yule: Recipes & Lore for the Winter Solstice*, and she's a regular contributor to the Llewellyn annuals. Follow her at www.facebook.com /SusanMoonwriterPesznecker and on Instagram as Susan Pesznecker.

Cerridwen Iris Shea was an urban witch and is now a coastal witch who focuses on kitchen, hearth, garden, and sea magic. She wrote for the Llewellyn annuals for sixteen years, took a break, and is delighted to be back. Visit her at cerridwenscottage.com and her blog, *Kemmyrk*, https://kemmyrk .wordpress.com.

Melissa Tipton is a licensed massage therapist, Reiki Master, and tarot reader. The author of *Living Reiki: Heal Yourself and Transform Your Life*, she helps clients unleash their inner awesomeness through her healing practice, Life Alchemy Massage Therapy. Learn more at getmomassage.com and www.yogiwitch.com.

Charlynn Walls holds a BA in anthropology, with an emphasis in archaeology. She is an active member of her local community. Charlynn teaches by presenting at various local festivals on a variety of topics. She continues to pursue her writing through articles for *Witches & Pagans* magazine and several of the Llewellyn annuals.

Tess Whitehurst teaches magical and intuitive arts in live workshops and via her online community and learning hub, the Good Vibe Tribe Online School of Magical Arts. An award-winning author, she's written eight books, which have been translated into eighteen languages. She's appeared on Bravo, Fox, and NBC, and her writing has been featured in *Writer's Digest* and *Spirit & Destiny* (in the UK) and on her popular website, tesswhitehurst.com.

Charlie Rainbow Wolf is happiest when she is creating something, especially if it's made from items that others have discarded. Pottery, writing, knitting, astrology, and tarot ignite her passion, but she happily confesses that she's easily distracted: life offers such wonderful things to explore! A recorded singer-songwriter and published author, she champions holistic living and lives in the Midwest with her husband and special-needs Great Danes. Visit her at www.charlierainbow.com.

Laura Tempest Zakroff is a professional artist, author, dancer, designer, and Modern Traditional Witch. She is the author of *Weave the Liminal*, *The Witch's Cauldron*, and *Sigil Witchery*, and the coauthor of *The Witch's Altar*. Laura blogs for Patheos and *Witches & Pagans*, contributes to *The Witches' Almanac*, and edited *The New Aradia: A Witch's Handbook to Magical Resistance*. Visit her at www.LauraTempestZakroff.com.

Spell Notes